Challenging Common Core Language Arts Lessons

ADVANCED CURRICULUM FROM THE
CENTER FOR GIFTED EDUCATION AT WILLIAM & MARY

Challenging Common Core Language Arts Lessons

Activities and Extensions for Gifted and Advanced Learners in
GRADE 7

ANITRA WALKER

William & Mary
School of Education

CENTER FOR GIFTED EDUCATION

P.O. Box 8795
Williamsburg, VA 23187

Prufrock Press Inc.
P.O. Box 8813
Waco, TX 76714-8813
Phone: (800) 998-2208
Fax: (800) 240-0333
http://www.prufrock.com

TABLE OF CONTENTS

INTRODUCTION

The Common Core State Standards (CCSS) for English Language Arts (ELA) are K–12 curriculum standards that describe the English language arts skills and concepts students need to develop for success in higher education and the 21st-century workplace.

The College and Career Readiness Anchor Standards are the basis of the ELA/literacy standards. They specify the core knowledge and skills needed, while grade-specific standards provide specificity. The ELA standards also establish guidelines for literacy in history/social studies, science, and technical subjects for grades 6–12.

With the adoption of the CCSS in nearly every state, gifted and advanced learners need opportunities to master grade-level standards and ELA skills and concepts with greater depth, rigor, and understanding. This book is one of a series of books developed in conjunction with the Center for Gifted Education at William & Mary intended to give gifted and advanced learners additional practice and activities to master and engage with the CCSS for ELA. Each book in the series is organized by the content standards in one grade.

The lessons in this book cover grade 7 ELA content. In grade 7, the standards are addressed in four domains:

- Reading Literature and Informational Text,
- Language,
- Speaking and Listening, and
- Writing.

PURPOSE

The lessons in this book were written with the assumption that a teacher has already introduced ELA content standards through primary curriculum sources. Reading, writing, and speaking activities enrich and extend current grade-level ELA content rather than accelerate students to above-grade-level content. Each lesson focuses on multiple content standards, due to the overlap of skills inherent in ELA activities, and provides additional support and enrichment for gifted and advanced learners.

BOOK AND LESSON STRUCTURE

This book is divided into four units, each of which contains multiple lessons. Each unit focuses on a particular theme and centers on the ideas related to the theme within literature and nonfiction texts. Within each unit, students will read, analyze, evaluate, and interpret poetry, short stories, and novels containing the theme. Students will demonstrate their growing understanding of the theme through various projects, narrative writing, informational writing, persuasive writing, and presentations.

Each lesson within a unit follows a predictable structure:

- The CCSS that are covered within the lesson are listed by number.
- Materials, including all student activity pages that are needed, are also listed. It is assumed students will have access to commonplace items such as pencils and paper, so the materials noted are those items that teachers will need to obtain/acquire in advance.
- Several required readings are available in the Appendix B: Text Exemplars and Sample Performance Tasks of the CCSS ELA document. (See additional information about text selection below.) It is anticipated that using these materials will allow for easy access to appropriate readings. In many cases, the readings that are used may come from the grade-level band above that of the grade level specified for the book.
- The lesson plan includes an estimate for the time it might take to complete the lesson; however, this will vary by teacher and classroom.
- The objectives highlight what students will learn or be able to do as a result of completing the lesson.
- An overview of the lesson's content provides a quick guide to the activities in which the students will be participating.
- A description of prior knowledge needed as a prerequisite for understanding the activities in a lesson is given. The teacher should be sure the students already have a working understanding of this content before beginning the lesson. Because the intended use of the activities is for students who have already mastered the stated standards, the teacher may want to preassess prior to having students complete the activities.
- The instructional sequence provides a detailed description of what the teacher and students will do during the lesson.
- The extension activities listed provide follow-up learning opportunities for students that go beyond the lesson to provide both additional enrichment and extension. Activities may be completed by individuals or groups, and may be completed at school or at home.
- At the end of each unit, a culminating essay is presented to provide closure and to assess students' synthesis of unit ideas.

THE SELECTION OF TEXT EXEMPLARS

The text exemplars selected for the book meet the specific criteria for high-ability learners suggested by Baskin and Harris (1980). These criteria (Center for Gifted Education, 2011) include:

- The language used in texts for the gifted should be rich, varied, precise, complex, and exciting.
- Texts should be chosen with a consideration of their open-endedness and their capacity to inspire thoughtful engagement.
- Texts for the gifted should be complex so that they promote interpretive and evaluative behaviors by readers.
- Texts for the gifted should help them develop problem-solving skills and acquire methods of productive thinking.
- Texts should provide characters as role models.
- Text types should cover a full range of materials and genres. (p. 15)

TOOLS FOR ANALYZING TEXTS

For several the activities in this book, it is recommended that the teacher have students complete the Literature Analysis Model (see Figure 1) as part of their first encounter with a text. However, teachers may want to use this model with other lessons. When students read the text for the first time, they should annotate it or use text coding (Harvey & Goudvis, 2007) as a metacognitive strategy to aid in comprehension. Once this marking of the text has occurred, the student should use the Literature Analysis Model and engage in a discussion about it (or selected portions) before progressing to other lesson activities.

The Literature Analysis Model encourages students to consider seven aspects of a selection they are reading: key words, tone, mood, imagery, symbolism, key ideas, and the structure of writing (Center for Gifted Education, 2011; McKeague, 2009; National Governors Association Center for Best Practices & Council of Chief State School Officers, 2010). After reading a selection, this model helps students to organize their initial responses and provides them with a basis for discussing the piece in small or large groups. Whenever possible, students should be allowed to underline and make notes as they read the material. After marking the text, they can organize their notes into the model.

Suggested questions for completing and discussing the model are:

- **Key words:** What words are important for understanding the selection? Which words did the author use for emphasis?
- **Important ideas:** What is the main idea of the selection? What are other important ideas in the selection?
- **Tone:** What is the attitude or what are the feelings of the author toward the subject of the selection? What words does the author use to indicate tone?

HANDOUT

Literature Analysis Model

Chosen or assigned text:	
Key words	
Important ideas	
Tone	
Mood	
Imagery	
Symbolism	
Structure of writing	

Figure 1. Literature Analysis Model. *Note.* Adapted from *Exploring America in the 1950s* (p. 10) by M. Sandling & K. L. Chandler, 2014, Waco, TX: Prufrock Press. Copyright 2014 by Center for Gifted Education. Adapted with permission.

- **Mood:** What emotions do you feel when reading the selection? How do the setting, images, objects, and details contribute to the mood?
- **Imagery:** What are examples of the descriptive language that is used to create sensory impressions in the selection?
- **Symbolism:** What symbols are used to represent other things?
- **Structure of writing:** What are some important characteristics of the way this piece is written? How do the parts of this selection fit together and relate to each other? How do structural elements contribute to the meaning of the piece?

After students have completed their Literature Analysis Models individually, they should compare their answers in small groups. These small groups may compile a composite model that includes the ideas of all members. Following the small-group work, teachers have several options for using the models. For instance, they may ask each group to report to the class, they may ask groups to post their composite models, or they may develop a new Literature Analysis Model with the class based on the small-group work. It is important for teachers to hold a whole-group discussion as the final aspect of implementing this model as a teaching-learning device. Teachers are also encouraged to display the selection on a document camera or overhead projector as it is discussed and make appropriate annotations. The teacher should record ideas, underline words listed, and call attention to student responses visually. The teacher should conclude the discussion by asking open-ended follow-up questions. For more information about analyzing literature, see Center for Gifted Education (2011).

GROUPING OPTIONS

The lessons in this book can be used for whole-group, small-group, and individual instruction.

Whole-Group Instruction

Teachers can use this book in one academic year in conjunction with the primary curriculum in a gifted education or advanced ELA class. All students would complete each lesson after being introduced to particular content standards. Teachers can integrate the lessons into the primary curriculum taught to a whole group and address higher order thinking questions through the lesson activities.

Small-Group Instruction

Teachers can use this book to differentiate learning in any ELA class by creating flexible student groups and giving students who need enrichment an opportunity for deeper understanding and engagement with a concept. Students can complete activities and practice at a self-guided pace with a partner or small group and engage in peer discussion, with or without directed supervision or intervention from the teacher.

Individual Instruction

The activities and questions in each lesson are a good way to determine individual understanding of a certain language arts concept on a deeper level.

AUTHOR'S RATIONALE FOR THE
TEXTS AND THEMES SELECTED

As an educator in the public school system for 14 years, I have learned to change my teaching methods in an effort to increase my students' understanding and success within the classroom. Over the years, I have created various lessons and used them in my classroom. I have made an attempt to compile some of the lessons my students found enjoyable during my teaching career, and I would like to share them with fellow educators. It was important to create lessons to allow the teacher to teach without the stress of finding materials to fit his or her curriculum. This work is developed for seventh-grade gifted students and is easily adaptable to any seventh-grade gifted classroom.

Your students will benefit from this text because it gives variety to your classroom assignments through the use of research, student-led discussion opportunities, and generation of text-based responses to questions. Students will work collaboratively and independently to meet classroom-activity learning goals you have set. Through the use of selected exemplar texts and planned activities, your students will be asked to address in-depth questions and provide well-defined arguments by linking knowledge and evidence together.

I hope you enjoy it! Happy teaching!

Conflict

This unit centers on the theme of struggling within oneself. Within the unit, students will read, analyze, evaluate, and interpret poems, short stories, and other texts and media that involve characters who battle internal conflict. Students will consider how characters' personal choices may or may not affect their futures, including their relationships and conflicts with others or society. Students will demonstrate their growing understanding of this theme through various projects, research, informational writing, persuasive writing, and poetry.

LESSON 1.1
Making Choices

Common Core State Standards

- RL.7.1
- RL.7.4
- SL.7.1c
- SL.7.1d

Materials

- Lesson 1.1 Poetry Analysis
- Lesson 1.1 Peer Evaluation
- Lesson 1.1 Rubric: Found Poem Presentation
- Student copies of "Stopping by the Woods on a Snowy Evening" by Robert Frost
- Student copies of "A Minor Bird" by Robert Frost
- Student copies of "The Road Not Taken" by Robert Frost (optional)
- Chart paper (one per pair of students)

Estimated Time

- 120 minutes

Objectives

In this lesson, students will:
- understand and analyze themes, actions, and literary devices in the context of a poem.

Content

Students will analyze poems through group discussion and create a "found" poem with their group members. Students will present their poems to the class for teacher evaluation and peer critique.

Prior Knowledge

Students should have experience with close reading, annotating, and rereading key passages for understanding. Students need to have knowledge of various types of figurative language, such as assonance, alliteration, consonance, imagery, and personification. Students should be able to recognize a poem's rhyme scheme and understand compare and contrast essay writing.

INSTRUCTIONAL SEQUENCE

1. Briefly review the difference between a theme and a moral. Students should understand that a theme is an overall concept/idea and a moral is a lesson learned through behavior or character. Guiding questions may include:
   - In the fairy tale "Little Red Riding Hood," what happened to Red as she traveled to her grandmother's house? Who did she meet? (Red was deceived or tricked. This could be a theme. She met a wolf, and by all natural instincts, she should have been afraid. She ignored her natural instincts of not speaking to the wolf and possibly running away; internal conflict.)
   - What did she find when she arrived to her grandmother's house? (The wolf was dressed as Red's grandmother; however, she noticed the eyes, ears, etc., were larger than usual. Again, she ignored her instincts and stayed. As a result, the wolf attacked; external conflict.)
   - What lesson did you learn from the story? (Do not talk to strangers. This could be the story's moral.)

2. Divide students into groups of two. Distribute one of the suggested Robert Frost poems—"Stopping by the Woods on a Snowy Evening" or "A Minor Bird"—to each group. "The Road Not Taken" can be substituted or added to the lesson at your discretion. You will want to divide the poems evenly among groups, as groups will converge later in the lesson to discuss their analyses of different poems.

3. Have each group perform a close reading of its selected poem. A close reading is when students circle new vocabulary, underline questionable sections, and create any notes or questions of their choosing on the side of the page pertaining to the text. Students may use their notes and questions for further discussion as the lesson progresses.

4. Distribute Lesson 1.1 Poetry Analysis for each group to complete.

5. Then, have each group join another group that analyzed a different poem (groups of two will become four). Groups should share what they have read and discuss the conflict found within the poems, as well as the use of figurative language, tone, and themes. Students should understand that nature is used as symbolism and is involved in the conflict of the speaker(s) in both poems:
   - The speaker in "Stopping by the Woods on a Snowy Evening" is conflicted by nature's beauty (the dark and beautiful woods) and the memory of what used to be. The speaker must decide between staying in the woods and leaving to fulfill other obligations.
   - The speaker in "A Minor Bird" is conflicted by nature, too. He is bothered by the bird's song and wants it to stop; however, he cannot understand why he wants such a beautiful song to end. The speaker has an internal conflict and an external conflict.

6. Have students divide into their original groups of two and distribute the additional poem(s) and chart paper to each group. With their partners, students will create a "found" poem, mixing and matching various lines from each poem. Students should decide which type of internal or external conflict will influence the speaker's emotions as he moves through the poem. They cannot delete or change words from the lines they use. In the final stanza, students should add their own words, keeping in mind that the stanza must follow the overall flow of the poem they have created. Once students have decided which lines to use from

each poem, have them write their found poem on chart paper. Encourage groups to give their poem a title that encompasses its overall theme. Distribute Lesson 1.1 Rubric: Found Poem Presentation before they begin.

> **Teacher's Note.** An Exceeds Expectation column has been added to the rubric to encourage students to push themselves beyond standard expectations. Very few students may rank in this column.

7. Have groups present their finished poems to the class. Distribute Lesson 1.1 Peer Evaluation for audience members to complete as each group presents.

> **Teacher's Note.** Before students complete Lesson 1.1 Peer Evaluation, it may be necessary to give an example of a constructive critique, for example, "Emily and James, I really liked your poem, but the rhyme scheme was not correct."

Extension Activities

Students may:
- create their own poems, mimicking the rhyme scheme of a self-selected Robert Frost poem; or
- create a cinquain or diamante poem based on the topic of nature.

LESSON 1.1
Poetry Analysis

Directions: With your partner, discuss your assigned poem by answering the corresponding questions. Then, complete the poetry analysis chart about the poem you read.

"Stopping by the Woods on a Snowy Evening" by Robert Frost

1. What do the woods and snow represent?

2. Reread stanza two. What is the dilemma of the speaker?

3. Reread the last stanza. What attracts the speaker to the woods?

"A Minor Bird" by Robert Frost

1. Identify the use of onomatopoeia in this poem.

2. Why does the bird irritate the speaker?

3. What could the bird and its song symbolize?

Challenging Common Core Language Arts Lessons: Grade 7 © Prufrock Press Inc.

Conflict

Poetry Analysis Chart

Title of Poem: _____

Type of Conflict: _____

Theme and Content	Response	Textual Evidence (Include Line Numbers)
What is the theme of the selection?		
What is the author's tone in this poem?		
Identify two types of figurative language used in this poem.		
Are smell, sight, touch, taste, or sound implied in the poem? How?		
What is the poem's rhyme scheme?		
Generate one discussion question that you and your partner will share with another group.		

LESSON 1.1
Peer Evaluation

Directions: Answer the following questions about your classmates' presentation. Be honest, and provide constructive criticism.

Group Members' Names:

1. Give one positive comment regarding the presentation you have just seen.

2. Give one comment critiquing the presentation you have just seen.

3. How could this group make a better project the next time?

4. Give your overall rating between 1 and 5 with 1 being the lowest: 1 2 3 4 5

Conflict

LESSON 1.1 RUBRIC
Found Poem Presentation

	Exceeds Expectations 5 points	Proficient 4 points	Developed 3 points	Emerging 2 points	Novice 1 point
Delegation of Responsibility	Each group member could go above and beyond to explain what information he or she was responsible for creating or locating.	Each group member could clearly explain what information he or she was responsible for locating.	Each group member could, with minimal prompting from peers, clearly explain what information he or she was responsible for locating.	Each group member could, with some prompting from peers, clearly explain what information he or she was responsible for locating.	One or more group members cannot clearly explain what information they were responsible for locating.
Figurative Language	Sensory details and figurative language create vivid images that contribute significantly to the meaning of the poem; sound devices, such as rhyme, alliteration, or onomatopoeia, are used effectively.	Sensory details and figurative language contribute to the meaning of the poem; sound devices, such as rhyme, alliteration, or onomatopoeia, are used effectively for the most part.	Sensory details and figurative language may be overused, underused, or inappropriate to the subject; sound devices, such as rhyme, alliteration, or onomatopoeia, may be overused or underused, or ineffective.	Sensory details and figurative language may not be appropriate to the subject; sound devices, such as rhyme, alliteration, or onomatopoeia, may fail to add to the meaning of the poem.	There is no use—or consistently confusing or inappropriate use—of sensory details, figurative language, or sound devices.
Word Choice	Word choice is vivid and exact throughout the poem.	Most word choices are precise.	Word choices may be vague, repetitive, or imprecise.	Word choices may be clear in some parts and unclear in others.	Words may be misused or unclear.
					_____ / 12

Conflict

Challenging Common Core Language Arts Lessons: Grade 7 © Prufrock Press Inc.
Permission is granted to photocopy or reproduce this page for single classroom use only.

LESSON 1.2
Lessons for the Future

Common Core State Standards

- RL.7.1
- RL.7.2
- RL.7.6
- W.7.7
- SL.7.1b
- SL.7.1c

Materials

- Lesson 1.2 Literature Analysis Model
- Lesson 1.2 Understanding the Text
- Lesson 1.2 Research Connection
- Lesson 1.2 Rubric: Research Presentation
- Student copies of "The Treasure of Lemon Brown" by Walter Dean Myers
- Student copies of "Thank You, Ma'am" by Langston Hughes
- Computer and Internet access
- Index cards (five per group)

Estimated Time

- 100 minutes (with additional time set aside for research)

Objectives

In this lesson, students will:
- understand an author's purpose, tone, and use of characterization; and
- use inferences drawn from a text in order to create a framework of questions that will guide further research on a topic.

Content

Students will focus on internal and external conflict, author's tone, purpose, and characterization as they analyze two short stories. Then, they will conduct a short research project exploring the causes and effects of homelessness in the United States or how the elderly are subjected to violence by youths in America.

Prior Knowledge

Students should have experience with close reading and rereading key passages for understanding. Students should understand how to conduct research, cite sources of information, and work within assigned groups.

INSTRUCTIONAL SEQUENCE

1. Tell students they will research one of two topics—causes and effects of youth homelessness or violence against the elderly—in an effort to connect real-life situations to fictional texts in which characters experience conflict. Ultimately, they will present their findings to the class through a PowerPoint, Prezi (https://prezi.com), or Glogster (http://www.glogster.com).

2. Divide students into groups of four based on their research preferences.

3. Then, have students read "The Treasure of Lemon Brown" by Walter Dean Myers (youth homelessness) or "Thank You, Ma'am" by Langston Hughes (violence against the elderly) according to their research preferences.

4. Distribute Lesson 1.2 Literature Analysis Model. For an initial analysis of their stories, have students complete and discuss the Literature Analysis Model with their groups. (See pp. 3–4 for more information about using the Literature Analysis Model.)

5. Afterward, distribute Lesson 1.2 Understanding the Text. Groups should complete the chart with all members' input. Consider allowing students to use chart paper and markers to create their charts.

6. Distribute five index cards to each group. Have students create their five research-based questions on the index cards and begin researching their topics, citing sources as necessary. Groups should consider narrowing their research to homelessness or violence against the elderly in a specific state or city. Guiding questions may include:
   - How many teens are found homeless every year?
   - What are some reasons why teens are found homeless every year?
   - Why is an elderly person subjected to violence by youths?
   - Is an elderly person more likely to be abused by a stranger or a caregiver?

Teacher's Note. Groups studying homelessness may find the following website useful: http://portal.hud.gov/hudportal/HUD. Groups studying violence against the elderly may find the following website useful: http://www.bjs.gov/index.cfm?ty=pbdetail&iid=5136.

7. After students have had sufficient time to analyze the text and research, students should begin creating their final product. Distribute Lesson 1.2 Research Connections and Lesson 1.2 Rubric: Research Presentation before they begin. Guiding questions may include:
   - As you completed your research, were there any similarities or differences found in the text regarding environment, social status, or family dynamics?
   - What types of external or internal conflicts are involved with your research topic?

8. As groups present, give peers a chance to ask questions and make comments where necessary. At the end of each presentation, peers should be allowed to give positive feedback and constructive criticism.

Extension Activities

Students may:
- write a new ending to "The Treasure of Lemon Brown" by Walter Dean Myers, or
- research homeless teens in America and write a letter to the local newspaper editor expressing an opinion about the subject.

LESSON 1.2
Literature Analysis Model

Directions: Complete this Literature Analysis Model about the short story you read.

Conflict

	Title and Author: _____
Key Words	
Important Ideas	
Tone	
Mood	
Imagery	
Symbolism	
Structure of Writing	

Note. Adapted from *Exploring America in the 1950s* (p. 10) by M. Sandling & K. L. Chandler, 2014, Waco, TX: Prufrock Press. Copyright 2014 by Center for Gifted Education. Adapted with permission.

LESSON 1.2
Understanding the Text

Directions: Using the short story you read, complete the following chart. Use complete sentences.

Title and Author: _____

Understanding the Text	Response	Textual Evidence
What does the title of the short story symbolize?		
Choose one type of literary device, such as symbolism, imagery, or dialogue, and explain its significance to the story's character(s).		
What examples of conflict are shown in this short story? Choose two types of conflict, such as man vs. man, man vs. himself, man vs. nature, or man vs. society. Explain their significance to the main character's situation.		
What is the overall theme of the story?		
Which type of characterization can be found in the short story? How does the selected characterization contribute to the understanding of the story's theme?		

Conflict

LESSON 1.2
Research Connections

Directions: What similarities did your group members find between the short story and the outside research on your selected topic? Complete the chart, recording three similarities and evidence to support them. Be sure to cite sources.

Research Fact	Textual Evidence	Connection Explanation (in Your Own Words)

Conflict

GROUP MEMBER NAMES: _____ DATE:_____

LESSON 1.2 RUBRIC
Research Presentation

	Exceeds Expectations 5 points	Proficient 4 points	Developed 3 points	Emerging 2 points	Novice 1 point
Ideas/ Research Questions	Researchers independently created and answered five questions/ideas regarding their researched topic; all questions were answered effectively.	Researchers independently identified and answered four of five questions/ ideas regarding their researched topic; questions were answered somewhat effectively.	Researchers independently identified and answered three of five questions/ ideas regarding their researched topic but lacked connection between the text and research.	Researchers independently identified and answered two of five questions/ ideas regarding their researched topic and lacked connection between the text and research.	Researchers independently identified and answered less than two questions/ideas regarding their researched topic; presentation lacked a logical sequence of information.
Delegation of Responsibility	Each group member could clearly explain what information the group needed and what information he or she was responsible for locating.	Each group member could clearly explain what information he or she was responsible for locating.	Each group member could, with minimal prompting from peers, clearly explain what information he or she was responsible for locating.	Each group member could, with prompting from peers, clearly explain what information she or she was responsible for locating.	One or more students in the group could not clearly explain what information they were responsible for locating.
Presentation	Speaker(s) maintained good eye contact with the audience; information was communicated well and the speaker used a clear voice.	Speaker(s) maintained good eye contact with the audience; information was communicated somewhat well and the speaker used a clear voice.	Speaker(s) did not always maintain good eye contact with the audience; information was communicated to the audience, but the speaker did not use a clear voice.	Speaker(s) did not maintain good eye contact with the audience; information was not communicated well, and the speaker did not use a clear voice.	Speaker(s) did not maintain good eye contact with the audience; information was not presented in a logical order, and the speaker mumbled during the presentation.
					_____ / 12

Conflict

LESSON 1.3

Rite of Passage

Common Core State Standards

- RL.7.1
- RL.7.2
- RL.7.6
- SL.7.1b
- SL.7.1c
- L.7.5a

Materials

- Lesson 1.3 Group Discussion Questions
- Lesson 1.3 Literature Analysis Model
- Lesson 1.3 Where Is John?
- Student copies of "By the Waters of Babylon" by Stephen Vincent Benét

Estimated Time

- 160 minutes

Objectives

In this lesson, students will:
- recognize theme, characters' actions and behaviors, and the use of biblical allusion in a text.

Content

Students will read and analyze a short story, connecting with the main character and his need to find his place in the world.

Prior Knowledge

Students should have experience with close reading, annotating and annotation symbols, and rereading key passages for understanding.

INSTRUCTIONAL SEQUENCE

1. Have students read "By the Waters of Babylon" by Stephen Vincent Benét.
2. Divide students into groups of two, and distribute Lesson 1.3 Group Discussion Questions and 2–3 index cards to each group. Students should answer the questions with their partner and then create two higher order thinking questions on the index cards.

Teacher's Note. Higher order thinking questions lead to challenge and reasoning; therefore, the following questions are not considered higher order:

- What is the conflict in the "By the Waters of Babylon"?
- Can you identify the parts of a short story?
- How many times did the bird whistle toward the window?

However, the following questions are examples of higher order questions:

- What is the significance of the conflict found between the two main characters? How does this conflict influence the story's plot?
- What clues found in the text show that the character John is in need of his independence?

3. Then, have groups meet with another group to discuss their higher order thinking questions (groups of two become four).
4. Afterward, have students analyze "By the Waters of Babylon" using Lesson 1.3 Literature Analysis Model. (See pp. 3–4 for additional information about using the Literature Analysis Model.)
5. Have students rejoin their groups of four. They will become detectives. The main character, John, has been exposed to various types of conflict—both external and internal—in his short quest to find out the true history of himself and his people. Distribute Lesson 1.3 Where Is John? Groups will complete the handout together and share their opinions based on textual evidence to find John's location.

Extension Activities

Students may:

- reread the last paragraph of the "By the Waters of Babylon," and in a brief paragraph, describe the importance of John's realization regarding the "men" who came before him to his future journey;
- locate examples of personification, metaphor, and simile found in the text, and explain their significance to the mood of the story and the character's conflict; or
- research rebuilding in New York after 9/11 (the following website may be useful: http://www.history.com/topics/911-rebuilding-of-ground-zero), and in a brief paragraph, discuss the significance of the rebuilding, comparing it to John's statement, "We must build again."

LESSON 1.3
Group Discussion Questions

Directions: Discuss and answer the following questions with your group members. Provide textual evidence to support your responses.

1. What is the significance of the title?

2. Identify an overall theme of "By the Waters of Babylon."

3. What if the Hill and Forest People coexisted in peace at one time? John considers the Hill People better than the Forest People. In your opinion, what could have driven them apart?

4. Before John leaves for his quest, his father tells him of "all things forbidden." Why does John decide to go east "in spite of the law"?

5. Explain John's dilemma when he says, "When the sun rose, I thought, 'My journey has been clean. Now I will go home from my journey.' But, even as I thought so, I knew I could not. If I went to the Place of the Gods, I would surely die, but, if I did not go, I could never be at peace with my spirit again." Briefly discuss John's internal struggle with himself.

6. Create two questions about the text, recording each on an index card. Then, exchange them with one of your group members. Answer each other's questions in a verbal exchange. When it is time to join another group, you will take these discussion questions with you.

LESSON 1.3
Literature Analysis Model

Directions: Complete this Literature Analysis Model about "By the Waters of Babylon" by Stephen Vincent Benét.

Conflict

"By the Waters of Babylon" by Stephen Vincent Benét	
Key Words	
Important Ideas	
Tone	
Mood	
Imagery	
Symbolism	
Structure of Writing	

Note. Adapted from *Exploring America in the 1950s* (p. 10) by M. Sandling & K. L. Chandler, 2014, Waco, TX: Prufrock Press. Copyright 2014 by Center for Gifted Education. Adapted with permission.

LESSON 1.3
Where Is John?

Directions: You and your group will become detectives as you analyze Stephen Vincent Benét's "By the Waters of Babylon." Some of the words and phrases in the text are distorted. Your group will have to decipher the real names of the terms described in the text and identify (using brief detail) the type of conflict (internal or external) experienced by John during his quest. Remember, John is a person with little knowledge of the world, and his father and spiritual traditions shape his beliefs. In the end, write down the real-life location (one of the 50 states) where these people, places, or things exist.

Place	Translation	Conflict
Ou-dis-sun	*Hudson River*	*External—John fought the currents to reach the Place of the Gods.*
Great Dead Places		
Place of the Gods		
Forest People		
Old Writings		
Dead God		

Where is John?

Conflict

LESSON 1.4

Alienation: Man Versus Society

Common Core State Standards

- RL.7.1
- RL.7.3
- RL.7.7
- W.7.6
- W.7.7
- SL.7.1c
- SL.7.1d

Materials

- Lesson 1.4 Literature Analysis Model
- Lesson 1.4 Compare and Contrast Organizer
- Lesson 1.4 Compare and Contrast Writing Template
- Lesson 1.4 Peer Review
- Lesson 1.4 Rubric: Compare and Contrast Essay
- Student copies of "Harrison Bergeron" by Kurt Vonnegut
- Film: *2081* (can be obtained from http://www.izzit.org/products/detail.php?video=2081)

Estimated Time

- 120 minutes

Objectives

In this lesson, students will:
- infer the traits, values, and motivations of the characters' actions and reasoning regarding contemporary beliefs and issues of justice within a text.

Content

Students will read and analyze a short story focusing on a character who is trying to find his place in society. Students will watch a film based on the text and discuss the similarities and differences between the text and film regarding the use of motifs and symbolism. Then, students will write a compare and contrast essay.

Prior Knowledge

Students should understand how to cite sources of information.

INSTRUCTIONAL SEQUENCE

1. Briefly review the plot of "By the Waters of Babylon" by Stephen Vincent Benét. Tell students they are going to read a similar short story, "Harrison Bergeron" by Kurt Vonnegut. Like John, Harrison Bergeron is a conflicted, alienated young man who wants to find his place in a dystopian society. Unlike John, his own self-discovery will end in tragedy.

2. Have students read "Harrison Bergeron" by Kurt Vonnegut. For an initial analysis of the story, have students complete Lesson 1.4 Literature Analysis Model. (See pp. 3–4 for more information about using the Literature Analysis Model.)

3. Invite students to pose their own discussion questions. Additional guiding questions may include:
   - How important is it to be an individual within a society?
   - "Harrison Bergeron" utilizes a communist social structure. It mentions changes to the Constitution to make everyone equal. Is it possible to make everyone "equal" within a society?
   - Describe Harrison's internal conflicts as he rebelled against society's handicap fixtures.
   - How did George's external conflicts prevent his rebellion against what he believed was right?

4. Divide students into pairs and distribute Lesson 1.4 Compare and Contrast Organizer. Have students watch the film *2081* and complete the handout.

5. Distribute Lesson 1.4 Compare and Contrast Writing Template. Tell students they will use their organizers and the writing template to develop a compare and contrast essay. Students ideas will vary; however, the essay should identify the conflict(s) found within the text and the film and describe how the conflict(s) influenced Harrison's actions of rebellion against society. Distribute Lesson 1.4 Rubric: Compare and Contrast Essay before they begin.

Teacher's Note. Make sure that students understand the use of internal and external conflicts regarding George and Harrison. These conflicts decide whether each will conform or rebel against society's rules (or handicaps).

6. After students develop first drafts of their essays, distribute Lesson 1.4 Peer Review. Have students work with partners to review and revise each other's drafts.

7. Then, have students produce final drafts for submission.

Extension Activities

Students may:
- view the music video for "Promises" by Nero (https://www.youtube.com/watch?v=llDik I2hTtk) and compare and contrast it to the film *2081*, using Lesson 1.4 Compare and Contrast organizer, noting the types of symbolism found in the film and video, themes, and conflict; or
- research a country of their choice and create a society of their own based on the selected country's current government (e.g., if China is selected, it is necessary to research and create a government similar to the Communist party) and present it to the class using Glogster

(https://www.glogster.com), Prezi (https://prezi.com), or PowerPoint. Students should create a flag for their society and a constitution, including the rights of its people, the jobs of its government, and how the laws are enforced. Students may create a more utopian or dystopian society at your discretion.

LESSON 1.4
Literature Analysis Model

Directions: Complete this Literature Analysis Model about "Harrison Bergeron" by Kurt Vonnegut.

Conflict

"Harrison Bergeron" by Kurt Vonnegut	
Key Words	
Important Ideas	
Tone	
Mood	
Imagery	
Symbolism	
Structure of Writing	

Note. Adapted from *Exploring America in the 1950s* (p. 10) by M. Sandling & K. L. Chandler, 2014, Waco, TX: Prufrock Press. Copyright 2014 by Center for Gifted Education. Adapted with permission.

NAME: _____ DATE: _____

LESSON 1.4
Compare and Contrast Organizer

Directions: After viewing the film and reading the short story, complete the triangles. Record similarities in the center triangle and differences in the left and right triangles. Include specific evidence as necessary.

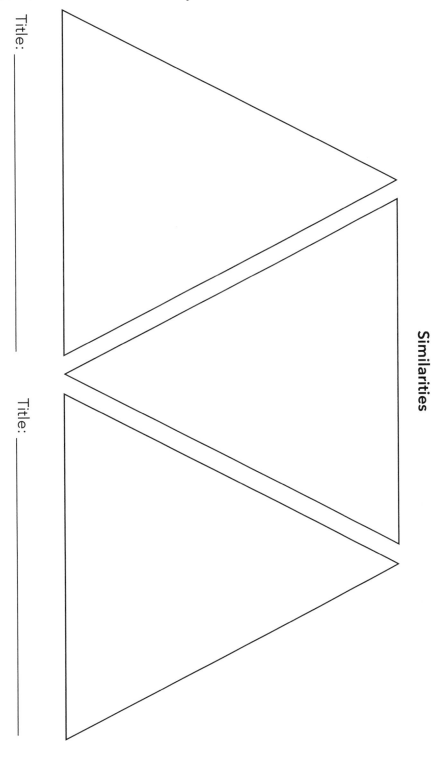

Title: _____

Title: _____

Similarities

Conflict

LESSON 1.4

Compare and Contrast Writing Template

Directions: Use the chart below to organize your compare and contrast essay.

Introduction	
Hook: Use an attention-grabbing first sentence about your topic. Consider a quote. Do not begin with: In this essay, I will talk about . . . I believe that . . . In my opinion . . . I think . . .	
Thesis: What is the main idea of your essay?	
What do the text and film have in common? What is the topic?	
How or where do the film and text differ? What is the topic?	
Body Similarities/Comparisons	
Create a topic sentence using the topic of comparison found in the film and short story.	
What is the reason for comparing this topic? Give examples to support your reasoning from the text and film.	

Elaborate on the examples given. Explain their significance.	
Transition to the next paragraph.	
What is the reason for comparing this topic? Give examples to support your reasoning from the text and film.	

Body Differences/Contrasts

Create a topic sentence using the topic of differences found in the film and short story.	
What is the reason for contrasting these topics? Give examples to support your reasoning from the text and film.	
Elaborate on the examples given. Explain their significance.	
Transition to the next paragraph. A transition sentence connects to the topic sentence of the next paragraph.	

Conclusion

Restate your comparisons/ contrasts. Tell the reader why you chose these topics. Reword or restate your thesis.	

Conflict

LESSON 1.4
Peer Review

Directions: After you review your partner's rough draft, answer the following questions and return the essay and this review sheet to him or her. Discuss your findings.

1. Did the writer use a hook within the introduction?   Yes   No

2. Did the writer have a solid thesis statement?   Yes   No

3. What is the thesis?   Yes   No

4. What is the centralized theme of the paper?   Yes   No

5. Do the facts of the paper coincide with the thesis?   Yes   No

6. Did the writer use parenthetical citations correctly?   Yes   No

7. List at least two quotes/statistics used by the writer to support his or her thesis.

8. Did the writer effectively describe the similarities and differences between the text and film?   Yes   No

9. In the conclusion, were the writer's ideas summarized effectively?   Yes   No

10. Finally, give some quality critique for the writer. How can he or she improve his or her paper for the final submission? Write your response below.

Conflict

LESSON 1.4 RUBRIC
Compare and Contrast Essay

	Exceeds Expectations 5 points	Proficient 4 points	Developed 3 points	Emerging 2 points	Novice 1 point
Focus or Thesis Statement	Thesis names the topic of the essay and outlines the main points to be discussed with a clear hook connected to a theme.	Thesis names the topic of the essay and outlines the main points to be discussed with a hook.	Thesis outlines some or all of the main points to be discussed but does not name the topic.	Thesis outlines vague main points to be discussed but does not name the topic.	Thesis does not name the topic and does not preview what will be discussed.
Support	Includes more than three pieces of textual evidence that support the thesis statement along with valid reasons for support.	Includes three or more pieces of textual evidence that support the thesis statement.	Includes three pieces of textual evidence that vaguely support the thesis statement.	Includes two pieces of textual evidence that support the thesis statement.	Includes one or fewer pieces of textual evidence with no support to the thesis statement.
Comparisons	Items are compared and contrasted clearly with valid reasons, which are logically tied to the main topic/theme of the paper.	Items are compared and contrasted clearly with valid reasons and support.	Items are compared and contrasted clearly, but adequate reasoning is not provided.	Items are compared and contrasted, but reasoning is very vague.	Only one item is discussed; author fails to create valid reasoning behind his or her purpose.
Transitions	A variety of well-organized transitions is used, and they clearly show the connection between paragraphs.	Well-organized transitions are used with some variety, and they clearly show the connection between paragraphs.	Transitions show the connections between paragraphs, but there is little variety.	Some transitions work well, but some connections between ideas are not entirely clear.	Transitions between paragraphs are unclear or nonexistent.
Closing Paragraph	Conclusion is strong and leaves the reader with a solid understanding of the writer's position; the thesis is effectively restated.	Conclusion leaves the reader with an understanding of the writer's position; the thesis is effectively restated.	Conclusion is recognizable, but it is not detailed; the thesis is restated.	Conclusion is too brief; the author fails to summarize points discussed in the essay or restate the thesis.	There is no conclusion.
					_____ / 20

Conflict

LESSON 1.5
Cultural Relationships and Transitions

Common Core State Standards

- RL.7.1
- RL.7.2
- RL.7.6
- W.7.7
- SL.7.1c

Materials

- Lesson 1.5 Literature Analysis Model
- Lesson 1.5 Conflict
- Lesson 1.5 Symbolism
- Lesson 1.5 Characterization
- Lesson 1.5 Metaphor
- Student copies of "Rules of the Game" and "Two Kinds" from *The Joy Luck Club* by Amy Tan
- Student copies of "Only Daughter" by Sandra Cisneros (optional)

Estimated Time

- 120 minutes

Objectives

In this lesson, students will:
- work in a group to analyze how one's culture influences behavior and relationships.

Content

Students will examine texts that exhibit cultural diversity and challenges faced by young women during their transitions into American society. Students will work in groups to identify textual evidence for literary devices, including conflict, symbolism, characterization, and metaphor.

Prior Knowledge

Students should have experience with close reading and rereading key passages for understanding. Students should be able to recognize characterization, theme, metaphor, and conflict.

Teacher's Note. If you choose, you may have students read all of *The Joy Luck Club* by Amy Tan or *Carmelo* by Sandra Cisneros before the lesson. However, due to the content and length, it is suggested that only excerpts be used for this lesson.

INSTRUCTIONAL SEQUENCE

1. Have students read "Rules of the Game" and "Two Kinds" from *The Joy Luck Club* by Amy Tan. *The Joy Luck Club* focuses on women's roles within Chinese culture and society along with the generational conflicts between Chinese-immigrant mothers and American-born daughters.

2. For an initial analysis of the novel, have students complete Lesson 1.5 Literature Analysis Model on one or both chapters. (See pp. 3–4 for more information about using the Literature Analysis Model.)

3. Discuss "Rules of the Game." Guiding questions may include:
   - What is the purpose of "the power of chess" according to Waverly Jong?
   - What was Waverly's fear of playing chess outside of her neighborhood? Why?
   - What do we know about Waverly Jong based on her descriptions of her neighborhood and family?

4. Discuss "Two Kinds." Guiding questions may include:
   - What does Jing-mei's mother want for her daughter?
   - What rivalry consists between the mothers of Waverly and Jing-mei?
   - Jing-mei's mother selected her to play the piano. What conflict is involved during the Jing-mei's lessons with Old Mr. Chong?

5. Divide students into four groups—conflict, symbolism, metaphor, and characterization. Distribute the appropriate handout to each group (see Materials list). Have groups complete the handout together. Monitor students during this activity and address any misunderstandings regarding the assigned task. Remind students to use textual evidence.

6. Once all groups are finished, have each group share with the class. Groups should explain their literary focus and their examples from the text with adequate explanations.

Extension Activities

Students may:
- read Sandra Cisneros's memoir "Only Daughter," and explain the family dynamics of a Mexican-American household told through the experiences of Cisneros in a brief essay;
- write a compare and contrast essay, comparing one of the family dynamics from *The Joy Luck Club* to own their household; or

Teacher's Note. "Only Daughter" is a short memoir by Sandra Cisneros. Cisneros was born to a Mexican-American mother and Mexican father and she describes what it was like to grow up as an only daughter in a family of six sons. As the only female, Cisneros was given an assigned role in the family with expectations. Throughout her adult life, she constantly sought the approval of her father. This memoir depicts her internal and external conflicts with herself, family, and culture.

- write an expository essay explaining the conflicts found within the mother-daughter relationships in "Rules of the Game" and "Two Kinds. "(Students should reread the scene where Waverly walks with her mother after winning many championships: "I wish you wouldn't do that, telling everybody I'm your daughter." They should also reread the scene after Jing-mei's recital fiasco when she argues with her mother and shouts, "Then I wish I weren't your daughter, I wish you weren't my mother.")

LESSON 1.5

Literature Analysis Model

Directions: Complete this Literature Analysis Model about a chapter from *The Joy Luck Club* by Amy Tan.

Conflict

	The Joy Luck Club: Chapter _____
Key Words	
Important Ideas	
Tone	
Mood	
Imagery	
Symbolism	
Structure of Writing	

Note. Adapted from *Exploring America in the 1950s* (p. 10) by M. Sandling & K. L. Chandler, 2014, Waco, TX: Prufrock Press. Copyright 2014 by Center for Gifted Education. Adapted with permission.

LESSON 1.5
Conflict

Directions: Complete the chart about conflict. Use textual evidence to support your answers.

Dictionary Definition of Conflict:	Group's Definition:

Question	Answer	Textual Evidence
What type of conflict is shown between Suyuan Woo and Jing-mei Woo? How is this conflict significant to the characters' development over the course of the story/novel?		
What type of conflict is shown between Lindo Jong and Waverly Jong? How is this conflict significant to the characters' development over the course of the story/novel?		
Explain the generational conflict found between the daughters and the mothers. How did this conflict influence the daughters' decisions?		

Conflict

LESSON 1.5

Symbolism

Directions: Complete the chart about symbolism. Use textual evidence to support your answers.

Dictionary Definition of Symbolism:	Group's Definition:	
Question	**Answer**	**Textual Evidence**
In "Rules of the Game," what is the significance of the "wind" as Waverly played chess with her opponent?		
In "Rules of the Game," interpret the following lines in your own words: "As I began to play, the boy disappeared, the color ran out of the room . . ."		
In "Two Kinds," what did the piano symbolize for Jing-mei? What did the piano symbolize for Jing-mei's mother?		

Question	Answer	Textual Evidence
In "Two Kinds," what is the significance of the title of the piano piece, "Pleading Child"?		
Interpret the following lines from "Two Kinds" in your own words: "And for the first time, or so it seemed, I noticed the piece on the right-hand side. It was called 'Perfectly Contented.' I tried to play this one as well. It had a lighter melody but with the same flowing rhythm and turned out to be quite easy. 'Pleading Child' was shorter but slower; 'Perfectly Contented' was longer but faster. And after I had played them both a few times, I realized they were two halves of the same song."		

Conflict

LESSON 1.5
Characterization

Directions: Complete the chart about characterization. Use textual evidence to support your answers.

Dictionary Definition of Characterization:	Group's Definition:	
Question	**Answer**	**Textual Evidence**
Describe the characteristics of Suyuan Woo and Jing-mei Woo? Consider their speech, personalities, and physical actions.		
Describe the characteristics of Lindo Jong and Waverly Jong. Consider their speech, personalities, and physical actions.		

LESSON 1.5
Metaphor

Directions: Complete the chart about metaphor. Use textual evidence to support your answers.

Dictionary Definition of Metaphor:	Group's Definition:	
Question	**"Two Kinds"**	**"Rules of the Game"**
Identify metaphors found in each chapter and explain the significance of the metaphors identified and why they are important to the text's central theme.		

Conflict

UNIT I

Culminating Essay Prompt

Directions: In this unit, you read about the internal struggles of various characters and how those struggles affected their life decisions. Discuss a choice that you were forced to make in your life that taught you a meaningful lesson. What did you learn from that lesson? Did you have any conflicting thoughts? As you write, compare yourself to one of the characters you learned about during this unit. Provide an example of the character's conflict and how that conflict compares to yours.

Conflict

A Tragic Flaw

This unit centers on the theme of the exhibition of a tragic flaw and how this characteristic can lead to a character's downfall. Within the unit, students will read, analyze, evaluate, and interpret texts, poems, and media in order to interpret the emotional growth and journey of a variety of characters. They will consider works by H. A. Guerber, William Carlos Williams, Rosemary Sutcliff, and Homer, as they explore how even heroes can be flawed. Students will demonstrate their growing understanding of this theme through various projects, discussions, and informational writing.

LESSON 2.1

Icarus Has Fallen

Common Core State Standards

- RL.7.1
- RL.7.4
- SL.7.1c
- SL.7.1d

Materials

- Lesson 2.1 Literature Analysis Model
- Lesson 2.1 "Musée des Beaux Arts" Analysis
- Lesson 2.1 "Landscape With the Fall of Icarus" Analysis
- Student copies of "Story of Daedalus and Icarus" from *The Story of the Greeks* by H. A. Guerber
- Student copies of "Musée des Beaux Arts" by W. H. Auden
- Student copies of "Landscape With the Fall of Icarus" by William Carlos Williams
- Student copies of *Black Ships Before Troy: The Story of the Iliad* by Rosemary Sutcliff
- Artwork: *Landscape With the Fall of Icarus* by Unknown (originally thought to be Pieter Bruegel)

Estimated Time

- 120 minutes

Objectives

In this lesson, students will:
- demonstrate the ability to interpret artwork and connect it to written text,
- make inferences, and
- determine the meaning of words and phrases as they are used in a poem.

Content

Students will read stories and poems and view artwork related to Daedalus and his son Icarus and discover why Icarus had wings fastened with wax. Using prior knowledge of figurative language and poetry terms, students will analyze poems and art, and discuss their findings as a class.

Prior Knowledge

Students should have experience with close reading and rereading key passages for understanding. Students should be able to identify stanzas and lines of poetry, recognize a poem's rhyme scheme, and understand various literary devices, including assonance, alliteration, consonance, imagery, and symbolism. Outside of class, students should begin reading *Black Ships Before Troy: The Story of the Iliad* by Rosemary Sutcliff in preparation for Lesson 2.2.

INSTRUCTIONAL SEQUENCE

1. Tell students that, throughout this unit, they will be exploring tragic flaws. A *tragic flaw*, or *hamartia*, is a flaw found within a character that brings forth his or her tragic downfall.

2. Display the painting *Landscape With the Fall of Icarus*. Ask students what they see in the painting. Guiding questions may include:
   - What do you think is happening in the painting? (Students may point out the farmer, shepherd, or fisherman, as well as the ships out on the water.)
   - Which colors does the painter use? What season do you think is being depicted? (Students may notice the colors appear bright and it might be springtime.)
   - Do you notice anything strange? (If necessary, point out the legs in the water in front of the ship.)

3. Ask students if they have ever heard the phrase "flying too close to the sun." Tell students they will be reading a story and poems related to the origin of this phrase.

4. Have students read "Story of Daedalus and Icarus" from *The Story of the Greeks* by H. A. Guerber and analyze the story using Lesson 2.1 Literature Analysis Model. You may wish to leave some of the boxes blank that may not be particularly relevant for this type of text. (See pp. 3–4 for additional information about using the Literature Analysis Model.) Guiding questions may include:
   - If Icarus was warned not to fly so close to the sun, why would he do it?
   - What is Icarus's tragic flaw? (Students should understand that his flaw could be seen as *hubris* or arrogance.)
   - Can you identify a type of conflict involved in the myth? Use textual evidence to support your answer.

5. Divide students into pairs. In each pair, give one student "Musée des Beaux Arts" by W. H. Auden, and give the other "Landscape With the Fall of Icarus" by William Carlos Williams.

6. Have students read the poems. As they read, if students find vocabulary they do not know, encourage them to discuss the word(s) with their partners.

7. Distribute Lesson 2.1 "Musée des Beaux Arts" Analysis and Lesson 2.1 "Landscape With the Fall of Icarus" Analysis according to students' readings. Have students work independently to complete the charts. Then, have students discuss their findings with their partners, focusing on human nature (with regard to Icarus falling unnoticed by anyone), the use of symbolism (such as springtime and its meaning of rebirth), and the changes in the author's tone in certain parts of the poems. Encourage students to seek textual evidence for their explanations.

8. Afterward, have groups share their findings with the rest of the class using the discussion questions they generated on the handouts.

9. Display the painting *Landscape With the Fall of Icarus* again. Students should look at the artwork and compare it to the poems. Guiding questions may include:

- Which visual elements of the painting are similar to or different than the poems by Auden and Williams?
- What is significant about the painting depicting springtime?
- What do you see regarding the use of lights and darks as a contrast in the painting? What is the significance?
- Did the artist evoke emotion in you as the viewer?
- What can you learn from Icarus's fall?

Extension Activities

Students may:

- read the Greek myth "Pandora's Box," identify Pandora's tragic flaw, and in a one-page response, answer the following: *What were the ramifications of Pandora's actions? What is the significance of the final element left inside the jar, and how does it relate to human nature?*; or
- read the Greek myth about Cassandra and Apollo, identify Cassandra's tragic flaw, and in a one-page response, answer the following: *Cassandra was beautiful and refused the advances of the god Apollo. As a result, she was punished. What was the punishment and how does the punishment of the "gift" influence the outcome of the Trojan War according to Greek mythology?*

LESSON 2.1
Literature Analysis Model

Directions: Complete this Literature Analysis Model about "Story of Daedalus and Icarus" by H. A. Guerber.

"Story of Daedalus and Icarus" by H. A. Guerber	
Key Words	
Important Ideas	
Tone	
Mood	
Imagery	
Symbolism	
Structure of Writing	

Note. Adapted from *Exploring America in the 1950s* (p. 10) by M. Sandling & K. L. Chandler, 2014, Waco, TX: Prufrock Press. Copyright 2014 by Center for Gifted Education. Adapted with permission.

LESSON 2.1
"Musée des Beaux Arts" Analysis

Directions: Complete the following chart about "Musée des Beaux Arts" by W. H. Auden. Use textual evidence to support your responses.

Question	Analysis	Textual Evidence
What is the poem's rhyme scheme?		
What is the author's tone?		
What do the first four lines of the poem mean?		

Question	Analysis	Textual Evidence
What examples of symbolism can you find in the poem?		
How is human nature portrayed in the poem?		
Identify three literary devices found in the poem.		
What are three questions you have about this poem? Generate three questions to address during class discussion.		

LESSON 2.1

"Landscape With the Fall of Icarus" Analysis

Directions: Complete the following chart about "Landscape With the Fall of Icarus" by William Carlos Williams. Use textual evidence to support your responses.

Question	Analysis	Textual Evidence
What is the poem's rhyme scheme?		
What is the author's tone?		
Why is it ironic that Williams chose to use springtime as the season?		
What do the last six lines of the poem mean?		

A Tragic Flaw

Question	Analysis	Textual Evidence
What examples of symbolism can you find in the poem?		
How is human nature portrayed in the poem?		
Identify three literary devices found in the poem.		
What are three questions you have about this poem? Generate three questions to address during class discussion.		

LESSON 2.2

Destruction

Common Core State Standards

- RL.7.1
- RL.7.7
- W.7.1
- W.7.2
- W.7.7
- SL.7.1c
- SL.7.1d

Materials

- Lesson 2.2 Literature Analysis Model
- Lesson 2.2 Character/Event Tracking
- Lesson 2.2 Discussion Strategy
- Lesson 2.2 Peer Evaluation
- Student copies of *Black Ships Before Troy: The Story of the Iliad* by Rosemary Sutcliff
- Film: *Maleficent*
- Index cards (two per student)
- Teacher's resources:
    - Athena: http://www.greekmythology.com/Olympians/Athena/athena.html
    - Hera: http://www.greekmythology.com/Olympians/Hera/hera.html
    - Aprhodite: http://www.greekmythology.com/Olympians/Aphrodite/aphrodite.html

Estimated Time

- 120 minutes

Objectives

In this lesson, students will:
- summarize a text, and
- determine two or more central ideas in a text and analyze their development.

Content

Students will read and analyze Rosemary Sutcliff's book *Black Ships Before Troy: The Story of the Iliad* in preparation for understanding Homer's *The Odyssey* in the next lesson. Students will relate the book to a recent film, analyze the story's characters and actions, and participate in a class discussion about the text.

Prior Knowledge

Students will need to have completed reading *Black Ships Before Troy: The Story of the Iliad* by Rosemary Sutcliff. Students will need experience interpreting vocabulary in context and using supporting evidence and textual details to draw conclusions about characters' traits and conflict. Students should understand how to conduct discussions with peers.

INSTRUCTIONAL SEQUENCE

1. Show an excerpt from the film *Maleficent* depicting the christening of the new princess. Maleficent, previously betrayed by the princess's father, arrives at the christening uninvited and, in act of vengeance, curses the princess. The king sends the princess away to live with three pixies. Ask students: *How is this scene similar to what you read in* Black Ships Before Troy? (Students may make connections between Eris being left out and introducing the golden apple to Athena, Hera, and Aphrodite, as well as Paris being sent away after the soothsayers' prophecy.)

2. Ask students what they know about the goddesses Athena, Hera, and Aphrodite. If necessary, provide a brief description of the goddesses (see Materials list).

3. Discuss the terms *jealousy* and *vengeance*. Guiding questions may include:
   - What does it mean to be jealous of someone and to seek vengeance?
   - For example, in Chapter 1, how do these terms reflect in Eris and Aphrodite's actions?
   - Is jealousy a flaw? If so, how?

4. Have students analyze at least one chapter of *Black Ships Before Troy: The Story of the Iliad* by Rosemary Sutcliff using the Literature Analysis Model. For an initial analysis of the novel, work with students to complete Lesson 2.2 Literature Analysis Model. You may wish to leave some of the boxes blank that may not be particularly relevant for this type of text. (See pp. 3–4 for more information about using the Literature Analysis Model.)

5. Distribute Lesson 2.2 Character/Event Tracking for students to complete in preparation for a fishbowl discussion. Encourage students to question the text by asking themselves probing questions about the characters' actions and emotions, the theme, the author's purpose, the types of conflict, and any unknown vocabulary. The handout asks them to develop two discussion questions in preparation for the class discussion, for example:
   - What is the significance of the black ships?
   - What did Achilles's armor symbolize to the Greeks and the Trojans? Why?

6. Have students record each of their questions on an index card and place them in a box.

7. Allow students to draw one or two questions from the box and sit in a fishbowl circle— some students seated in an inner circle and some in an outer circle—for discussion. Have each student in the inner circle partner with a student in the outer circle. Outer circle students will track the discussion on Lesson 2.2 Discussion Strategy and then rate their partner's performance with Lesson 2.2 Peer Evaluation.

8. Then, have students in the inner and outer circles switch to conclude the discussion.

> ***Teacher's Note.*** During the fishbowl discussion, allow students in the inner circle to read a selected question and one member within the circle may answer at a time. Others in the circle may add additional information to the response, but they must remember to show discussion etiquette of not talking over one another and showing respect for other's ideas and opinions. Students placed in the outer circle are to watch, listen, and document. Outer circle students should have one member assigned to them so they may track the discussion.

Extension Activities

Students may:

- write a short essay about how the hubristic character traits of Achilles and his personal choices resulted in his eventual demise; or
- research the Trojan War and write a narrative from the perspective of Helen of Troy regarding her involvement in the war.

LESSON 2.2
Literature Analysis Model

Directions: Complete this Literature Analysis Model about *Black Ships Before Troy: The Story of the Iliad* by Rosemary Sutcliff.

Black Ships Before Troy: The Story of the Iliad **by Rosemary Sutcliff**	
Key Words	
Important Ideas	
Tone	
Mood	
Imagery	
Symbolism	
Structure of Writing	

A Tragic Flaw

Note. Adapted from *Exploring America in the 1950s* (p. 10) by M. Sandling & K. L. Chandler, 2014, Waco, TX: Prufrock Press. Copyright 2014 by Center for Gifted Education. Adapted with permission.

LESSON 2.2
Character/Event Tracking

Directions: Record significant characters you are introduced to in *Black Ships Before Troy*. Write down the action (choice) and outcome (result) of the character's choice. Then, decide the type of characterization for each character:

1. **Flat character:** A character who shows little emotion during the story and is defined by few traits.
2. **Round character:** A character who has many sides including various internal conflicts.
3. **Static character:** A character who stays the same through the course of the story.
4. **Dynamic character:** A character who shows significant changes through the course of the story.

Character	Action (Choice)	Outcome (Result)	Characterization (Dynamic, Static, Round, or Flat) and Textual Evidence

Character	Action (Choice)	Outcome (Result)	Characterization (Dynamic, Static, Round, or Flat) and Textual Evidence

After completing the chart above, create two questions about any character, event, or item you choose. What do you not understand about a character's actions or about the way a character or event is portrayed in the text?

1.

2.

LESSON 2.2
Discussion Strategy

Directions: Observe and record you partner's contributions to the discussion in the inner circle. When your partner answers a question, record his or her response and write down your response to your partner's answer, noting whether you agree or disagree.

Partner's Name: _____

Main Idea of the Discussion and Partner's Response	Personal Response Regarding the Discussion
Example Question: *In Chapter 2, Thetis held Achilles around the ankle as she dipped him in the river. How is this an example foreshadowing Achilles's fate?* **Partner's Response:** *I think . . . because . . . and in the text . . .*	**My Response:** *I agree/disagree because . . .*

Challenging Common Core Language Arts Lessons: Grade 7 © Prufrock Press Inc.

A Tragic Flaw

LESSON 2.2
Peer Evaluation

Directions: After the discussion, evaluate your partner's participation. Circle a rating of 1–5, with 1 as the lowest score. Provide comments if necessary.

Partner's Name: _____

Details	Rating	Comments
Asked a question pertaining to the text or characters found within the text.	5 4 3 2 1	
Answered questions effectively using textual evidence.	5 4 3 2 1	
Utilized an effective rebuttal to an opposing opinion.	5 4 3 2 1	
Maintained discussion etiquette. He or she did not talk over anyone else and waited until the other person finished before responding.	5 4 3 2 1	

A Tragic Flaw

LESSON 2.3

A Hero's Road

Common Core State Standards

- RL.7.1
- W.7.3
- W.7.3a
- SL.7.1c
- SL.7.1d

Materials

- Lesson 2.3 Literature Analysis Model
- Lesson 2.3 Hero's Journey
- Lesson 2.3 Greek Gods and Goddesses
- Lesson 2.3 Hero in the News Chart
- Student copies of "Perseus and Medusa"
- Student copies of "Perseus and Andromeda"
- Student copies of *The Odyssey* by Homer
- Newspaper clippings depicting heroes within the community
- Teacher's resources:
  - "Greek Myths" (http://www.greekmyths-greekmythology.com/c/greek-myths)
  - "What Is a Myth?" (http://www.pbs.org/mythsandheroes/myths_what.html)

Estimated Time

- 120 minutes (with additional time set aside for research)

Objectives

In this lesson, students will:
- determine the theme or central idea of a text and analyze its development over the course of the text, and
- summarize a text.

Content

Students will read an epic poem and myths involving Perseus's quests and Odysseus's heroic actions. Then, students will explore archetypal hero characteristics of fictional characters and real-life heroes found in the news.

Prior Knowledge

Students will need to have read Books 9–10 of *The Odyssey* by Homer. Students will need experience making inferences and using supporting evidence and textual details to draw conclusions. Students should have some knowledge the archetypal traits of a hero and how to recognize characters' traits and conflict.

INSTRUCTIONAL SEQUENCE

1. Have students analyze at least one book of *The Odyssey* by Homer using Lesson 2.3 Literature Analysis Model. You may wish to leave some of the boxes blank that may not be particularly relevant for this type of text. (See pp. 3–4 for more information about using the Literature Analysis Model.)

2. Explain the difference between myths and legends and their significance to the epic poem *The Odyssey*.

Teacher's Note. PBS (http://www.pbs.org/mythsandheroes/ myths_what.html) can assist in the explanation of Greek drama, theatre, myths, legends, and heroes.

3. Ask students what they know about the words *hero*, *heroism*, and *epic*. Guiding questions may include:
   - In your opinion, what makes a hero?
   - What are the characteristics of a hero?
   - Do you know of any examples of heroes in literature, movies, or real life?
   - *The Odyssey* is considered an epic poem. Why do you think that is?

4. Invite students to identify their interpretation of heroic characteristics. Ask students to identify a fictional character who may possess the identified characteristic, for example:
   - **Fearless:** Katniss Everdeen from *The Hunger Games*
   - **Caring:** Frodo Baggins from *The Lord of the Rings*
   - **Loyal:** Samwise Gamgee from *The Lord of the Rings*

   Note that all three of these characters volunteered to complete an action/quest for the sake of others. Their honor/nobility would be a tragic flaw because they all lost friends or put their friends' lives in danger because they were followed or "looked up to" by others.

5. Provide students with an introduction to archetypal traits and tell them to look for such traits as they read the stories of Perseus.

6. Distribute the myths "Perseus and Medusa" and "Perseus and Andromeda." Have students annotate as they read, paying special attention to things they may not understand.

7. Discuss the myths. Guiding questions may include:
   - How was Perseus called to adventure?
   - What trials did Perseus face during his quest?
   - How did Perseus's quest change when he met Andromeda?

> **Teacher's Note.** Archetypal traits are characteristics of heroes. According to *The Hero With a Thousand Faces* by Joseph Campbell, mythical/epic heroes found across the world have the same key events in common with a hero's journey or cycle of events: The hero receives a call to adventure, gets assistance from a supernatural being, departs on a quest, is subjected to trials, deals with a crisis, completes the quest, and returns home to a new life.

- Andromeda's mother Cassiopeia bragged about her daughter's beauty. How did this trait result in Andromeda's potential downfall?
- Medusa killed many who tried to end her life. How did her underestimation of Perseus's skills contribute to her demise?

8. Distribute Lesson 2.3 Hero's Journey for students to complete. Discuss students' responses with the whole class.
9. Distribute Lesson 2.3 Greek Gods and Goddesses. This is necessary for the final product and should only take about 30 minutes.
10. Afterward, divide students into groups of three and assign them a newspaper article. The newspaper articles should depict various periods of time and show examples of heroism within the community. Distribute Lesson 2.3 Hero in the News Chart for groups to complete.
11. Discuss groups' responses. Guiding questions may include:
    - Where did you see evidence of heroism in the article?
    - Give an example from the article to support your response.
    - What heroic trait would you use to describe the person?

Extension Activities

Students may:
- interview someone in their family who possesses a heroic trait: *What makes them a hero? How do they influence the family or society?*; or
- create a narrative in which they are a real-life hero, written in first person with a setting, full character description, conflict, and resolution.

LESSON 2.3
Literature Analysis Model

Directions: Complete this Literature Analysis Model about a book from *The Odyssey* by Homer.

A Tragic Flaw

	The Odyssey: Book _____
Key Words	
Important Ideas	
Tone	
Mood	
Imagery	
Symbolism	
Structure of Writing	

Note. Adapted from *Exploring America in the 1950s* (p. 10) by M. Sandling & K. L. Chandler, 2014, Waco, TX: Prufrock Press. Copyright 2014 by Center for Gifted Education. Adapted with permission.

LESSON 2.3
Hero's Journey

Directions: Track Perseus's and Odysseus's journeys as they each find their way home. Which hero characteristics do they each have? Do they share common characteristics? Complete the hero cycle below with information about Perseus's heroic journey. Then, complete the second hero cycle with information about Odysseus's heroic journey.

Perseus

Heroes' Characteristics Found in Perseus:
1. *Brave*

2.

3.

Challenging Common Core Language Arts Lessons: Grade 7 © Prufrock Press Inc.

A Tragic Flaw

Odysseus

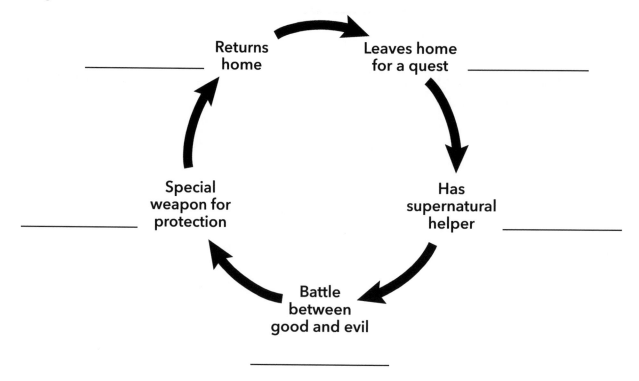

Heroes' Characteristics Found in Odysseus:
1. *Cunning*

2.

3.

LESSON 2.3
Greek Gods and Goddesses

Directions: Research each god and goddess of Greek mythology and complete the following chart. An example has been provided. After you complete the chart, answer the questions regarding your own characteristics.

God/Goddess	Symbol	Weapon	Flaw
Athena	*Wisdom, battle strategy, overall skill*	*Sword/shield*	*Prideful*
Aphrodite			
Apollo			
Ares			
Artemis			
Demeter			
Hermes			
Hera			
Hades			
Poseidon			
Zeus			

1. Which Greek god/goddess represents you?

2. Why does he or she represent you? What are your characteristics?

3. What symbol would represent you? Why?

A Tragic Flaw

LESSON 2.3
Hero in the News Chart

Directions: Using a newspaper article, complete the chart about a real-life hero.

A Tragic Flaw

Newspaper and Publication Date: _____	
Title and Writer of the Story: _____	
Summarize the conflict in the story.	
Who was the hero?	
What made this person a hero in the eyes of the newspaper reporter and readers?	
Which characteristics of a hero did this person possess?	
Did the hero exhibit a tragic flaw? Or, what changes in circumstances could make this hero a "tragic hero"?	

LESSON 2.4

Vengeance Versus Vindication

Common Core State Standards

- RL.7.1
- RL.7.5
- SL.7.1c
- SL.7.1d

Materials

- Lesson 2.4 Literature Analysis Model
- Lesson 2.4 Event Summary Chart
- Lesson 2.4 Symbolism and Theme
- Student copies of *The Odyssey* by Homer
- Index cards (two per student)

Estimated Time

- 120 minutes

Objectives

In this lesson, students will:
- use textual evidence to support analysis of what a text says explicitly, and
- draw inferences from a text.

Content

Students will continue studying the epic poem *The Odyssey* and will engage in discussions regarding the characters, the use of symbolism, the use of deities as a motif within the poem, and the exploration of Odysseus as a tragic hero.

Prior Knowledge

Students will need to have read Books 11–13 and 22–23 of *The Odyssey* by Homer. They should understand Odysseus's reasons for leaving home and embarking on his journey. Students should have knowledge of the hero's cycle and archetypal characteristics of a hero. Students should be able to analyze literature and make inferences using supporting textual evidence.

Teacher's Note. Ask students to utilize sticky notes to record questions or comments throughout the readings and discussions.

Divide students into groups of two during the independent readings. As students read, inform them they should make notes of characters and their actions, conflicts, and the use of a deity as a motif found throughout the text.

INSTRUCTIONAL SEQUENCE

1. Have students analyze at least one book of *The Odyssey* by Homer using Lesson 2.3 Literature Analysis Model. You may wish to leave some of the boxes blank that may not be particularly relevant for this type of text. (See pp. 3–4 for more information about using the Literature Analysis Model.)

2. Have students develop two questions they have about the text and record them on index cards. Students should generate higher level questions (e.g., Why did Odysseus's men expect the Cyclops to give them hospitality in Book 9 when they had taken his food without asking?) rather than lower level questions (e.g., Why did the Cyclops kill Odysseus's men? Who thought Aeolus gave Odysseus riches?).

3. First, have students share their questions with a partner and then switch cards with another group. The group receiving the cards should discuss the questions and put an answer on the back of the card before returning it to the initial group.

4. Distribute Lesson 2.4 Event Summary Chart. Students should discuss the events of Books 11–13 and 22–23 in logical order with a partner and write down the important elements that shaped Odysseus and his fate. Guiding questions may include:
   - What examples can you find of Odysseus and his men struggling with temptation and/or physical appeal?
   - How was the journey to the Land of the Dead a test of morality on behalf of Odysseus? Provide an example of the conflicts encountered by Odysseus during this journey.

5. Afterward, students should be divided into pairs again. Distribute Lesson 2.4 Symbolism and Theme. Each group should complete the activity and discuss its contents with a partner.

6. Discuss students' findings. Guiding questions may include:
   - Odysseus returned home in disguise with the assistance of Athena to retrieve his home, his wife, and his life as he knew it. He dispensed justice without mercy to the suitors. How did Odysseus's bow become a symbol of justice?
   - Why was it important for the 12 maids who betrayed Odysseus to clean his home before their death? What did the maids symbolize for Odysseus?
   - What did Odysseus mean when he said, "Bring sulfur, nurse, to scour all this pollution—bring me fire too, so I can fumigate the house"?

Extension Activities

Students may:

- read Aristotle's *Poetics* and write a short essay using evidence from *Poetics* and *The Odyssey* to answer: *How are women's roles in Greek dramas portrayed differently than men?*; or
- read Aristotle's *Poetics* and write a short essay using evidence from *Poetics* and *The Odyssey* to answer: *According to Aristotle, tragedy is evoked by pity and fear. How are these characteristics seen in Odysseus's journey home?*

LESSON 2.4
Literature Analysis Model

Directions: Complete this Literature Analysis Model about a book from *The Odyssey* by Homer.

	The Odyssey: Book _____
Key Words	
Important Ideas	
Tone	
Mood	
Imagery	
Symbolism	
Structure of Writing	

Note. Adapted from *Exploring America in the 1950s* (p. 10) by M. Sandling & K. L. Chandler, 2014, Waco, TX: Prufrock Press. Copyright 2014 by Center for Gifted Education. Adapted with permission.

LESSON 2.4
Event Summary Chart

Directions: Record the important events as they happen in each book of *The Odyssey*.

A Tragic Flaw

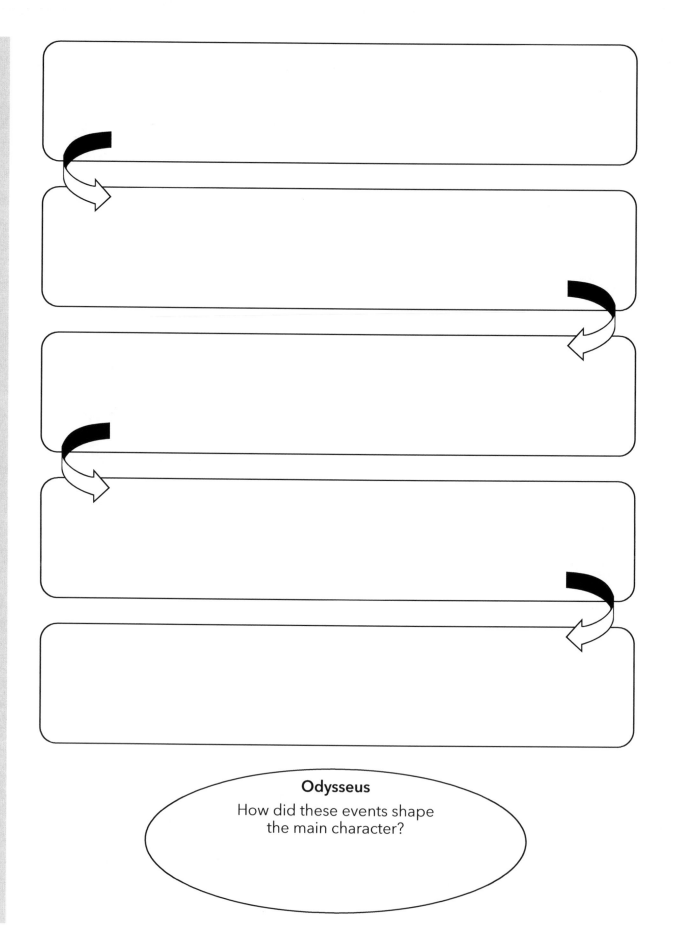

Odysseus

How did these events shape
the main character?

LESSON 2.4
Symbolism and Theme

Directions: Complete the following chart. Explain each symbol's meaning, and cite textual evidence. Then, list examples of the theme of a tragic flaw using textual evidence.

Symbol	Meaning	Textual Evidence
The Land of the Dead		
Odysseus's Bow		
The Sea		
Ithaca		
Athena		
Theme		
Tragic Flaw *Find examples of this theme in the text, and explain it using Odysseus's characteristics and actions.*		

A Tragic Flaw

LESSON 2.5
Tempting Fate

Common Core State Standards

- RL.7.1
- RL.7.5
- RL.7.7
- SL.7.1c
- SL.7.1d

Materials

- Lesson 2.5 Literature Analysis Model
- Lesson 2.5 Poetry Analysis
- Lesson 2.5 Art and Music Analysis
- Lesson 2.5 Compare and Contrast Brainstorm
- Lesson 2.5 Rubric: Compare and Contrast Essay
- Student copies of *The Odyssey* by Homer
- Student copies of "Siren Song" by Margaret Atwood
- Student copies of "Ithaka" by Constantine P. Cavafy
- Artwork: *Ulysses and the Sirens* by J. W. Waterhouse
- Music: "Epic Siren Music - Queen of the Sea" by Peter Crowley (https://www.youtube.com/watch?v=IlEk4G_Afmo)
- Music: "Greatest Battle Music of All Times - Sirens' Call [Epic Score]" (optional; https://youtube.com/watchv=abYpXSeTCWo)

Estimated Time

- 180 minutes

Objectives

In this lesson, students will:
- compare and contrast a written story, drama, or poem to its multimedia version, and
- analyze the effects of techniques unique to the medium.

Content

Students will continue studying the epic poem *The Odyssey* by reading related poems. They will also view art and listen to music that relate to Odysseus's journey and evaluate, compare, contrast, and discuss. Then, they will write a compare and contrast essay.

Prior Knowledge

Students will need to have read Books 1 and 14 of *The Odyssey* by Homer. They should have knowledge of Odysseus's past encounters on his journey. Students should have knowledge of the hero's journey archetype and characteristics of a hero. Students must be able to analyze poetry for meaning and figurative language and to compare and contrast text.

INSTRUCTIONAL SEQUENCE

1. Have students analyze at least one book of *The Odyssey* by Homer using Lesson 2.3 Literature Analysis Model. You may wish to leave some of the boxes blank that may not be particularly relevant for this type of text. (See pp. 3–4 for more information about using the Literature Analysis Model.)
2. Have students read "Siren Song" by Margaret Atwood and "Ithaka" by Constantine P. Cavafy. Tell students that Books 12–14 of *The Odyssey* include references to the Sirens and Book 1 describes life in Ithaka.

Teacher's Note. It may be necessary to explain the connection between Book 1 and the poem "Ithaka." Homer introduces the characters, an implied theme, and plot immediately to the reader. He allows the reader to see the society and traditions in order to provide a visual of what Odysseus sees and what he left behind.

3. Distribute Lesson 2.5 Poetry Analysis for students to complete in pairs. Discuss students' responses. Guiding questions may include:
   - Where did you see evidence of temptation in the texts read today? Give an example from the text to support your response.
   - How can a character's temptation exhibit a tragic flaw?

4. Display *Ulysses and the Sirens* by J. W. Waterhouse. Distribute Lesson 2.5 Art and Music Analysis. Students should look at the artwork and compare the art to "Siren Song" through written analysis and class discussion.
5. Then, play "Epic Siren Music - Queen of the Sea" or "Greatest Battle Music of All Times - Sirens' Call [Epic Score]." Students should relate either song's musical score to the poem "Siren Song." Students should pay attention to the tone of the piece and the blending of the musical instruments as they complete the handout. Discuss students' findings. Guiding questions may include:
   - How are the voices/chants used as musical instruments?
   - What do the voices signify in reference to the Sirens?
   - Why would the Sirens be considered "queens" of the sea?

6. Have students complete a compare and contrast essay involving the poems, musical scores, the painting, or the text read during this lesson. Distribute Lesson 2.5 Compare and Contrast Brainstorm and Lesson 2.5 Rubric: Compare and Contrast Essay before they begin.

Extension Activities

Students may:

- summarize Lines 25–35 of "Ithaka" by Constantine P. Cavafy in their own words and create an explanation of the poem's stanzas using Book 1 of *The Odyssey*; or
- revisit Book 14 of the Odyssey, and write a paragraph response using textual evidence to answer: *As Odysseus talks to Eumaeus, Odysseus discusses his quest for fame, glory, treasure, and honor. How are these characteristics examples of hubris?*

LESSON 2.5
Literature Analysis Model

Directions: Complete this Literature Analysis Model about a book from *The Odyssey* by Homer.

A Tragic Flaw

	The Odyssey: Book _____
Key Words	
Important Ideas	
Tone	
Mood	
Imagery	
Symbolism	
Structure of Writing	

Note. Adapted from *Exploring America in the 1950s* (p. 10) by M. Sandling & K. L. Chandler, 2014, Waco, TX: Prufrock Press. Copyright 2014 by Center for Gifted Education. Adapted with permission.

LESSON 2.5
Poetry Analysis

Directions: Use the poems "Siren Song" and "Ithaka" to answer the following questions. You may reference *The Odyssey*.

Understanding the Text	Response	Textual Evidence
Choose one type of literary device and explain its significance to "Siren Song." How does imagery add to the use of symbolism within the poem?		
How does "Ithaka" imitate *The Odyssey*?		
Identify the audience for each poem. Who are the speakers and why are they important to the poems?		
How did each piece contribute to your understanding of *The Odyssey*?		

A Tragic Flaw

LESSON 2.5
Art and Music Analysis

Directions: Complete the following questions about the art you viewed and the music you listened to.

1. Describe the painting. What is happening in the painting? Look at the use of colors. Look at the characters in the painting. What do you notice?

2. What are the similarities between the visual elements of the painting and "Siren Song" by Margaret Atwood? Use textual evidence to support your response.

3. Did the artist evoke emotion in you as the viewer? Use textual evidence to support your response.

A Tragic Flaw

4. Complete the following chart using the musical score and "Siren Song" by Margaret Atwood.

Musical Score	"Siren Song" by Margaret Atwood
Tone:	Tone:
Musical Shifts:	Emotional Shifts:
Instruments Heard:	Alliteration:
Symbolism:	Symbolism:
How did it make you feel?	How did it make you feel?
Who is the audience?	Who is the audience?

LESSON 2.5

Compare and Contrast Brainstorm

Directions: Choose a poem, piece of music, or painting from this lesson to compare and contrast. Brainstorm your ideas before creating a formal essay.

Topic 1: _____   **Topic 2:** _____

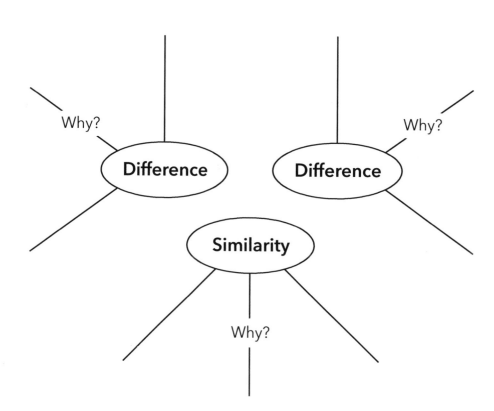

NAME:_____ DATE:_____

LESSON 2.5 RUBRIC
Compare and Contrast Essay

	Exceeds Expectations 5 points	Proficient 4 points	Developed 3 points	Emerging 2 points	Novice 1 point
Focus or Thesis Statement	Thesis names the topic of the essay and outlines the main points to be discussed with a clear hook connected to a main idea.	Thesis names the topic of the essay and outlines the main points to be discussed with a hook.	Thesis outlines some or all of the main points to be discussed but does not name the topic.	Thesis outlines vague main points to be discussed but does not name the topic.	Thesis does not name the topic and does not preview what will be discussed.
Support	Includes more than three pieces of textual evidence that support the thesis statement along with valid reasons for support.	Includes three or more pieces of textual evidence that support the thesis statement.	Includes three pieces of textual evidence that vaguely support the thesis statement.	Includes two pieces of textual evidence that support the thesis statement.	Includes one or fewer pieces of textual evidence with no support to the thesis statement.
Comparisons	Items are compared and contrasted clearly with valid reasons, which are logically tied to the main topic/ theme of the paper.	Items are compared and contrasted clearly with valid reasons and support.	Items are compared and contrasted clearly, but adequate reasoning is not provided.	Items are compared and contrasted, but reasoning is very vague.	Only one item is discussed; author fails to create valid reasoning behind his or her purpose.
Transitions	A variety of well-organized transitions is used, and they clearly show the connection between paragraphs.	Well-organized transitions are used with some variety, and they clearly show the connection between paragraphs.	Transitions used show the connections between paragraphs, but there is little variety.	Some transitions work well, but some connections between ideas are not entirely clear.	Transitions between paragraphs are unclear or nonexistent.
Closing Paragraph	Conclusion is strong and leaves the reader with a solid understanding of the writer's position; the thesis is effectively restated.	Conclusion leaves the reader with an understanding of the writer's position; the thesis is effectively restated.	Conclusion is recognizable, but it is not detailed; the thesis is restated.	Conclusion is too brief; the author fails to summarize points discussed in the essay or restate the thesis.	There is no conclusion.
					_____ / 20

A Tragic Flaw

NAME:_____ DATE:_____

UNIT II
Culminating Essay Prompt

Directions: In this unit, you explored human nature and how a tragic flaw can lead to decisions that can impact one's life forever. In an expository essay, discuss a tragic flaw that you possessed. How did others react to you? How did you recognize the flaw? What changes did you make in order to improve yourself? Use at least one character you read about during this unit and textual evidence to support your explanations.

Challenging Common Core Language Arts Lessons: Grade 7 © Prufrock Press Inc.
Permission is granted to photocopy or reproduce this page for single classroom use only.

UNIT III

Civil Rights

This unit centers on the theme of obtaining civil rights for all citizens. Within the unit, students will read, analyze, evaluate, and interpret texts written by historical figures, such as Franklin D. Roosevelt, Nelson Mandela, Langston Hughes, and Dr. Martin Luther King, Jr. Students will explore civil rights, journeying from the Montgomery Bus Boycott in Alabama and the Civil Rights Movement in the United States to South Africa's Apartheid Movement. Students will demonstrate their growing understanding of the theme through various projects, class discussions, informational writing, and persuasive writing.

LESSON 3.1

Freedom Writer

Common Core State Standards

- RL.7.1
- RI.7.3
- RI.7.6
- W.7.9
- SL7.1c
- SL.7.1d

Materials

- Lesson 3.1 Literature Analysis Model
- Lesson 3.1 SOAPStone Analysis
- Lesson 3.1 Rubric: Compare and Contrast Essay
- Student copies of "I Have a Dream" speech by Dr. Martin Luther King, Jr.
- Student copies of "I've Been to the Mountaintop" speech by Dr. Martin Luther King, Jr.
- Video: "Martin Luther King, Jr.: Mini Biography" (http://www.biography.com/people/martin-luther-king-jr-9365086/videos/martin-luther-king-jr-mini-biography-490925 635609)

Estimated Time

- 150 minutes

Objectives

In this lesson, students will:
- determine an author's point of view or purpose and explain how it is conveyed in the text through the use of allusions and allegorical references.

Content

Students will be introduced to the speeches of Dr. Martin Luther King, Jr. and his use of persuasive language. Students will then write a compare and contrast essay.

Prior Knowledge

Students will need experience analyzing thematic elements in a text and using supporting evidence and textual details to draw conclusions. Students should have some understanding of the three dimensions of persuasive speech: pathos, ethos, and logos. Students should recognize these dimensions and be able to utilize examples of them in a persuasive or compare and contrast essay.

INSTRUCTIONAL SEQUENCE

1. Introduce Dr. Martin Luther King, Jr., showing the video biography.
2. Assess students' knowledge of logos (logic and reasoning), pathos (emotion), and ethos (ethics). Tell students that they are used to convince audiences to agree or change their opinions to match the speaker's opinion. Ask students to assess the following statements:
   - As your doctor, I can assure you that this is the best treatment for you. (Ethos.)
   - You deserve to have a better school and I know you all will vote for me as class president. (Pathos.)
   - The data show that 90% of the students enrolled in our middle school have cell phones. (Logos.)

3. Have students read King's "I Have a Dream" speech. For an initial analysis of the speech, have students complete Lesson 3.1 Literature Analysis Model. (See pp. 3–4 for more information about using the Literature Analysis Model.)
4. Divide students into groups of three and distribute Lesson 3.1 SOAPStone Analysis for groups to complete. Discuss students' responses.

Teacher's Note. SOAPSTone is an outlining strategy that allows students to organize the structure of a speech into their own thoughts before they begin writing an essay. The strategy focuses on the speaker, the time/place of the speech, the intended audience of the speech, the reason behind writing the speech, the overall subject of the text, and the attitude of the author.

5. Read the following excerpt from King's "I Have a Dream" speech, and ask students to identify whether it is an example of ethos, pathos, or logos:

   Let us not seek to satisfy our thirst for freedom by drinking from the cup of bitterness and hatred. We must forever conduct our struggle on the high plane of dignity and discipline. We must not allow our creative protest to degenerate into physical violence. Again and again we must rise to the majestic heights of meeting physical force with soul force.

   The marvelous new militancy which has engulfed the Negro community must not lead us to a distrust of all White people, for many of our White brothers, as evidenced by their presence here today, have come to realize that their destiny is tied up with our destiny. And they have come to realize that their freedom is inextricably bound to our freedom. We cannot walk alone.

   Then, ask students: *How is this excerpt an example of a call for peace?*

6. Have students read "I've Been to the Mountaintop" and complete another copy of Lesson 3.1 SOAPStone Analysis with their groups. Discuss students' responses. Guiding questions may include:

- Identify three allusions found in Dr. King's speech. What do they represent and why are they important to Dr. King's plight?
- What does King mean by "economic withdrawal"? Is this an example of logos, pathos, or ethos?
- Why did Dr. King read a letter to the crowd written by a young White girl after he had been stabbed? Is this an example of logos, pathos, or ethos?

7. Ask students to differentiate or compare King's "I Have a Dream" and "I've Been to the Mountaintop" speeches and their significance. There is a difference in speech and emotion in the two selections. Have students describe why there is such a difference and for what purpose. (Students should draw the conclusion that the audience may have something to do with the speech's difference; however, answers may vary.)
8. Afterward, have students write an essay comparing and contrasting the two speeches and their uses of persuasive language.

Extension Activities

Students may:
- research Jim Crow laws and write a brief essay on the differences between the laws then and now; or
- create a Venn diagram comparing/contrasting the Jim Crow laws (South) to the pass laws (South Africa).

LESSON 3.1
Literature Analysis Model

Directions: Complete this Literature Analysis Model about "I Have a Dream" by Dr. Martin Luther King, Jr.

"I Have a Dream" by Dr. Martin Luther King, Jr.	
Key Words	
Important Ideas	
Tone	
Mood	
Imagery	
Symbolism	
Structure of Writing	

Note. Adapted from *Exploring America in the 1950s* (p. 10) by M. Sandling & K. L. Chandler, 2014, Waco, TX: Prufrock Press. Copyright 2014 by Center for Gifted Education. Adapted with permission.

LESSON 3.1
SOAPStone Analysis

Directions: Using the speech you read, complete the chart. Provide textual evidence for your explanations in the right column.

SOAPSTone	Explanation	Textual Evidence
Speaker *Who is the speaker?*		
Occasion *When was the speech written and why?*		
Audience *Who is the intended audience?*		
Purpose *What is the reason behind the speech?*		
Subject *What is the topic?*		
Tone *What is the author's tone?*		

Note. Adapted from *SOAPSTone: A Strategy for Reading and Writing* by O. Morse, 2016, retrieved from http://apcentral.collegeboard.com/apc/public/preap/teachers_corner/45200.html.

Civil Rights

LESSON 3.1 RUBRIC
Compare and Contrast Essay

	Exceeds Expectations 5 points	Proficient 4 points	Developed 3 points	Emerging 2 points	Novice 1 point
Focus or Thesis Statement	Thesis names the topic of the essay and outlines the main points to be discussed with a clear hook connected to a main idea.	Thesis names the topic of the essay and outlines the main points to be discussed with a hook.	Thesis outlines some or all of the main points to be discussed but does not name the topic.	Thesis outlines vague main points to be discussed but does not name the topic.	Thesis does not name the topic and does not preview what will be discussed.
Support	Includes more than three pieces of textual evidence that support the thesis statement along with valid reasons for support.	Includes three or more pieces of textual evidence that support the thesis statement.	Includes three pieces of textual evidence that vaguely support the thesis statement.	Includes two pieces of textual evidence that support the thesis statement.	Includes one or fewer pieces of textual evidence with no support to the thesis statement.
Comparisons	Items are compared and contrasted clearly with valid reasons, which are logically tied to the main topic/theme of the paper.	Items are compared and contrasted clearly with valid reasons and support.	Items are compared and contrasted clearly, but adequate reasoning is not provided.	Items are compared and contrasted, but reasoning is very vague.	Only one item is discussed; author fails to create valid reasoning behind his or her purpose.
Transitions	A variety of well-organized transitions is used, and they clearly show the connection between paragraphs.	Well-organized transitions are used with some variety, and they clearly show the connection between paragraphs.	Transitions used show the connections between paragraphs, but there is little variety.	Some transitions work well, but some connections between ideas are not entirely clear.	Transitions between paragraphs are unclear or nonexistent.
Closing Paragraph	Conclusion is strong and leaves the reader with a solid understanding of the writer's position; the thesis is effectively restated.	Conclusion leaves the reader with an understanding of the writer's position; the thesis is effectively restated.	Conclusion is recognizable, but it is not detailed; the thesis is restated.	Conclusion is too brief; the author fails to summarize points discussed in the essay or restate the thesis.	There is no conclusion.
					_____ / 20

LESSON 3.2

Peaceful Protest

Common Core State Standards

- RI.7.6
- W.7.4
- W.7.9
- SL7.1c
- L.7.5c

Materials

- Lesson 3.2 Literature Analysis Model
- Lesson 3.2 Persuasive Language Analysis
- Lesson 3.2 Compare and Contrast Brainstorm
- Lesson 3.2 Rubric: Compare and Contrast Essay
- Student copies of "Letter From Birmingham Jail" by Dr. Martin Luther King, Jr.
- Student copies of "An Appeal for Law and Order and Common Sense" by Paul Hardin, Eugene Blackshleger, Milton L. Grafman, Joseph A. Durick, Nolan B. Harmon, Soterios D. Gouvellis, George M. Murray, C. C. J. Carpenter, J. T. Beale, Edward V. Ramage, and Earl Stallings
- Student copies of the First and Fourteenth Amendments to the U.S. Constitution
- Colored pencils (blue, red, and green for each student)
- Index cards (two per student)

Estimated Time

- 150 minutes

Objectives

In this lesson, students will:
- identify the use of persuasive speech and trace various themes and actions throughout a text in an effort to understand an author's purpose.

Content

Students will focus on the use of persuasive language in two letters in an effort to pinpoint the authors' purpose and tone. They will explore the privileges they enjoy within the U.S. today compared to people of color who protested for their civil rights during the 1960s. Then, students will write a compare and contrast essay.

Prior Knowledge

Students will need to have prior knowledge of elements found in persuasive speeches (ethos, pathos, and logos) and recognizing an author's tone and purpose. Students should be familiar with the U.S. Constitution and what it means to the American people.

INSTRUCTIONAL SEQUENCE

1. Ask the class to list rights or privileges they enjoy as American citizens. Help students understand that before they were born, African American citizens were denied some of those rights; ask them how they would feel if they were in that situation.

Teacher's Note. If you feel comfortable, the topic of present-day racial injustices and protest examples may be brought into this lesson with sensitivity.

2. Have students read the First and Fourteenth Amendments to the U.S. Constitution. Assist students in the interpretation of the content by focusing on key statements from each. Guiding questions may include:
   - "No state shall make or enforce any law which shall abridge the privileges or immunities of citizens of the United States; nor shall any state deprive any person of life, liberty, or property, without due process of law; nor deny to any person within its jurisdiction the equal protection of the laws." What does this quote mean in reference to your rights as an American citizen?
   - "Congress shall make no law respecting an establishment of religion, or prohibiting the free exercise thereof; or abridging the freedom of speech, or of the press, or the right of the people peaceably to assemble, and to petition the Government for a redress of grievances." What does this quote mean in reference to Dr. Martin Luther King, Jr.'s actions during the Civil Rights Movement? What does the statement mean to you today?

3. Have students read King's "Letter From Birmingham Jail." Ask them to use three colored pencils to mark ethos in blue, pathos in red, and logos in green as they move through the text. For an initial analysis of the speech, have students complete Lesson 3.2 Literature Analysis Model. (See pp. 3–4 for more information about using the Literature Analysis Model.)

4. Then, distribute "An Appeal for Law and Order and Common Sense." Have a student read (or have students take turns reading) the clergy's letter aloud as the rest of the class searches the text for important ideas, tone, and important vocabulary, recording questions they have about the text in the margins. Ask them to use three colored pencils to mark ethos in blue, pathos in red, and logos in green as they move through the text.

5. Discuss students' findings. Guiding questions may include:
   - What is King's purpose? What is the clergymen's purpose?
   - What is King's tone? What is the clergymen's tone?

6. Distribute Lesson 3.2 Persuasive Language Analysis for students to complete. Discuss students' responses.

7. Then, distribute two index cards to each student. On their index cards, have students prepare two questions regarding either of the letters, King's actions during the Civil Rights Movement, or any Amendments to the Constitution. Guiding questions may include:
   - Were King's First Amendment rights violated when he was arrested?
   - What rights does King believe he has a citizen of the United States?
   - What was the purpose of the clergymen's letter? What did they hope to accomplish in the Southern community regarding King's supporters and protesters?

8. Have students participate in a shared-inquiry discussion using the index card questions. Place students in a large circle. Read a question to the group to prompt discussion. Students may answer questions or agree or disagree with other students' responses using textual evidence. Continue asking new questions based on the group's responses.

> **Teacher's Note.** A shared-inquiry discussion allows students to agree or disagree with each other using text-based responses and build upon the responses with new questions. Students listen and respond, and the group leader (teacher) asks questions based on the direction of the discussion. Every student must answer at least once with a complete response using evidence from the text.

9. Afterward, have them write an essay comparing and contrasting the letters. Distribute Lesson 3.2 Compare and Contrast Brainstorm and Lesson 3.2 Rubric: Compare and Contrast Essay before they begin.

Extension Activities

Students may:
- research the Montgomery Bus Boycott, focusing on the role the Women's Political Council played and what it used to persuade bus riders, and then, create a flyer to persuade classmates to make a change to the classroom/school's rules using logos, pathos, or ethos; or
- research the influence of Rosa Parks on the Civil Rights Movement and write a poem depicting Parks's feelings as she was arrested for refusing to give up her seat.

LESSON 3.2
Literature Analysis Model

Directions: Complete this Literature Analysis Model about "Letter From Birmingham Jail" by Dr. Martin Luther King, Jr.

"Letter From Birmingham Jail" by Dr. Martin Luther King, Jr.	
Key Words	
Important Ideas	
Tone	
Mood	
Imagery	
Symbolism	
Structure of Writing	

Note. Adapted from *Exploring America in the 1950s* (p. 10) by M. Sandling & K. L. Chandler, 2014, Waco, TX: Prufrock Press. Copyright 2014 by Center for Gifted Education. Adapted with permission.

LESSON 3.2
Persuasive Language Analysis

Directions: After reading King's letter and the clergymen's letter, complete the chart using textual evidence. Be prepared to discuss your responses with the class.

Persuasive Elements of Writing	Argument Against King's Plight According to the Clergy	Argument for King's Plight According to King
Pathos: Audience Appeal		
Logos: Logic of Breaking the Law and Getting Arrested		
Ethos: Credibility		

LESSON 3.2
Compare and Contrast Brainstorm

Directions: Analyze the texts written by Dr. Martin Luther King, Jr. and the clergymen. Decipher the common theme found in both letters and write it in the similarity section. Then, compile differences using textual evidence in preparation for your essay.

Dr. Martin Luther King, Jr.	The Clergymen
Similarity	
Differences	

LESSON 3.2 RUBRIC
Compare and Contrast Essay

	Exceeds Expectations 5 points	Proficient 4 points	Developed 3 points	Emerging 2 points	Novice 1 point
Focus or Thesis Statement	Thesis names the topic of the essay and outlines the main points to be discussed with a clear hook connected to a main idea.	Thesis names the topic of the essay and outlines the main points to be discussed with a hook.	Thesis outlines some or all of the main points to be discussed but does not name the topic.	Thesis outlines vague main points to be discussed but does not name the topic.	Thesis does not name the topic and does not preview what will be discussed.
Support	Includes more than three pieces of textual evidence that support the thesis statement along with valid reasons for support.	Includes three or more pieces of textual evidence that support the thesis statement.	Includes three pieces of textual evidence that vaguely support the thesis statement.	Includes two pieces of textual evidence that support the thesis statement.	Includes one or fewer pieces of textual evidence with no support to the thesis statement.
Comparisons	Items are compared and contrasted clearly with valid reasons, which are logically tied to the main topic/theme of the paper.	Items are compared and contrasted clearly with valid reasons and support.	Items are compared and contrasted clearly, but adequate reasoning is not provided.	Items are compared and contrasted, but reasoning is very vague.	Only one item is discussed; author fails to create valid reasoning behind his or her purpose.
Transitions	A variety of well-organized transitions is used, and they clearly show the connection between paragraphs.	Well-organized transitions are used with some variety, and they clearly show the connection between paragraphs.	Transitions used show the connections between paragraphs, but there is little variety.	Some transitions work well, but some connections between ideas are not entirely clear.	Transitions between paragraphs are unclear or nonexistent.
Closing Paragraph	Conclusion is strong and leaves the reader with a solid understanding of the writer's position; the thesis is effectively restated.	Conclusion leaves the reader with an understanding of the writer's position; the thesis is effectively restated.	Conclusion is recognizable, but it is not detailed; the thesis is restated.	Conclusion is too brief; the author fails to summarize points discussed in the essay or restate the thesis.	There is no conclusion.
					_____ / 20

Civil Rights

LESSON 3.3
Apartheid

Common Core State Standards

- RL.7.1
- RI.7.3
- RI.7.6
- W.7.4
- W.7.9

Materials

- Lesson 3.3 Literature Analysis Model
- Lesson 3.3 Civil Rights Concept Organizer
- Lesson 3.3 Mini Research Project
- Lesson 3.3 Rubric: Mini Research Project
- Lesson 3.3 Rubric: Persuasive Essay
- Student copies of Chapter 11 from *A Long Walk to Freedom* by Nelson Mandela
- Video: "Nelson Mandela: Mini Biography" (http://www.biography.com/people/nelson-mandela-9397017/videos/nelson-mandela-mini-biography-596206659979)
- Computer and Internet access

Estimated Time

- 120 minutes (with additional time set aside for research)

Objectives

In this lesson, students will:
- research civil rights in the Southern United States and in South Africa.

Content

Students will compare and contrast the Civil Rights Movement in the U.S. to the anti-apartheid movement in South Africa in an effort to understand the lack of civil rights granted to those of color. Then, students will conduct a mini research project on the Civil Rights Movement in the U.S. and the effects of apartheid in South Africa and present their findings to the class.

Prior Knowledge

Students will need to have read Chapter 11 from *A Long Walk to Freedom* by Nelson Mandela. Students will need to understand modes of persuasion (logos, pathos, and ethos) and have experience using supporting evidence to draw conclusions regarding an author's tone and purpose.

INSTRUCTIONAL SEQUENCE

1. Have students analyze Chapter 11 from *A Long Walk to Freedom* using Lesson 3.3 Literature Analysis Model. You may wish to leave some of the boxes blank that may not be particularly relevant for this type of text. (See pp. 3–4 for more information about using the Literature Analysis Model.)

2. Distribute Lesson 3.3 Civil Rights Concept Organizer, explaining to students that they will use the handout to explore their meaning and the actual meaning of *civil rights*. Model how to complete the organizer using a think-aloud strategy. Allow students 5–7 minutes to complete the handout.

3. Ask students about their knowledge regarding South Africa and its people and the importance of Nelson Mandela and Willem de Klerk. Give a brief introduction to these men and their influence on South Africa's government.

Teacher's Note. The Nobel Prize website gives wonderful inspirational accounts of both men's influence on the abolishment of Apartheid and their work toward peace in South Africa: https://www.nobelprize.org/nobel_prizes/peace/laureates/1993.

4. Show Nelson Mandela's biography video. Inform students that as they watch the video to pay attention the involvement of Mandela in the anti-apartheid movement and role that Willem de Klerk plays in Mandela's freedom.

5. Have students research the time period of the Civil Rights Movement in the U.S. and the establishment of the Jim Crow laws, and apartheid in South Africa and the creation of the pass laws. Distribute Lesson 3.3 Mini Research Project and Lesson 3.3 Rubric: Mini Research Project. Suggest to students they may use any of Dr. Martin Luther King's speeches to assist them in completing their project and to remember to cite information.

Teacher's Note. Lesson 3.3 Mini Research Project includes a list of possible resources for students to use as they complete their research project. The resources are suggestions identified by the author and, because URLs may be updated or changed and availability of books may be limited, alternative resources may be used at your discretion.

6. Have students present their information to the class using PowerPoint, Glogster (https://www.glogster.com), or Prezi (https://prezi.com). Students can create pamphlets if there is no computer access. As students present, have them answer questions posed by classmates.

7. Afterward, ask students to take a position for or against a current law or situation they would like to change, brainstorm, and write a persuasive essay based on their position. Distribute Lesson 3.3 Rubric: Persuasive Essay before they begin. Suggested topics might include:
   - Should movies/music have age ratings for audiences?
   - Should teens receive driver's licenses at the age of 16?
   - Should students have their lockers searched if there is probable cause?
   - Should middle school students attend school year-round?
   - Are curfews necessary for teenagers?
   - Should there be a regulation of cell phone usage on middle school campuses?

Extension Activities

Students may:
- read the first 3–4 paragraphs of Chapter 52 from Nelson Mandela's *A Long Walk to Freedom* and create a Venn diagram, comparing how Dr. Martin Luther King, Jr.'s and Mandela's confinements in jail are similar and different; or
- read Nelson Mandela's "I Am Prepared to Die" speech (starting with "Our fight is against real . . .") and, in a chart, compare his use of persuasive language (logos, pathos, and ethos) to that of King's "I Have a Dream" speech.

LESSON 3.3
Literature Analysis Model

Directions: Complete this Literature Analysis Model about a chapter from *A Long Walk to Freedom* by Nelson Mandela.

	A Long Walk to Freedom: Chapter _____
Key Words	
Important Ideas	
Tone	
Mood	
Imagery	
Symbolism	
Structure of Writing	

Note. Adapted from *Exploring America in the 1950s* (p. 10) by M. Sandling & K. L. Chandler, 2014, Waco, TX: Prufrock Press. Copyright 2014 by Center for Gifted Education. Adapted with permission.

LESSON 3.3
Civil Rights Concept Organizer

Directions: Complete each of the boxes based on the term *civil rights*.

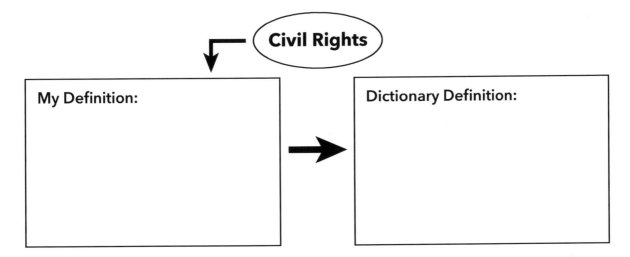

| My Definition: | Dictionary Definition: |

Your Ideas About Maintaining One's Civil Rights:

| Example: | **Historical Figures Who Advocated for Civil Rights:** | **Related Words/Phrases:** |

Nonexample:

A Sentence Using the Phrase *Civil Rights*:

LESSON 3.3
Mini Research Project

Directions: Research Apartheid in South Africa and the Civil Rights Movement in the Southern United States. As you research these topics, find information regarding the laws of the time period (the Jim Crow laws and the pass laws), the effects of the laws on the people, and key historical figures who participated in the fight for civil rights and against Apartheid. Focus on a time period between 1950–1975 in the United States and 1950–1995 in South Africa.

1. Create your presentation using Glogster (https://www.glogster.com), Prezi (https://prezi.com), or PowerPoint.

2. You *must* include a works cited section and have *at least five* sources, including one book. Here are a few websites and books to begin your search:
   - "Civil Rights Movement (1954–1985)" by PBS (http://www.pbs.org/black-culture/explore/civil-rights-movement)
   - "The Anti-Apartheid Movement's Untold Stories" by Tell Me More (http://www.npr.org/2012/01/19/145454148/the-anti-apartheid-movements-untold-stories)
   - "Youth in the Civil Rights Movement" by Library of Congress (https://www.loc.gov/collections/civil-rights-history-project/articles-and-essays/youth-in-the-civil-rights-movement)
   - "The Rise and Fall of Jim Crow" by PBS (http://www.pbs.org/wnet/jimcrow)
   - *Causes and Consequences of the End of Apartheid* by Catherine Bradley
   - *The Jim Crow Laws and Racism in American History* by David K. Fremon

3. End your presentation with a self-reflection of your thoughts as you researched these topics, connecting your research to the texts you have read during this unit as well as current social issues.

Civil Rights

LESSON 3.3 RUBRIC
Mini Research Project

	Exceeds Expectations 5 points	Proficient 4 points	Developed 3 points	Emerging 2 points	Novice 1 point
Connections to Content	Shows outstanding connections to content through research, covering the most important facts and details of the event or person's life, with additional connections to other people and events.	Shows excellent connections to content through research, covering the most important facts and details of the event or person's life.	Shows good connections to content through research, covering the important facts and details of the event or person's life.	Shows some connections to content through research, covering some facts and details of the event or person's life, but facts are weak.	Shows no connections to content through research; does not cover the facts and details of the event or person's life effectively.
Evidence of Research and Knowledge	Outstanding evidence of research and depth of content knowledge.	Clear evidence of research and depth of content knowledge.	Evidence of research and some content knowledge.	Some evidence of research but little content knowledge.	No evidence of research and little to no depth of content knowledge.
Bibliography	Has six or more sources, all cited correctly.	Has five sources, all cited correctly.	Has four or more sources; almost all are cited correctly.	Has three sources; all are cited correctly.	Has one source or fewer cited correctly.
Sentence Structure, Grammar, Mechanics, and Spelling	Sentence structure is outstanding, greatly contributing to the effectiveness of the writing with no errors in grammar, mechanics, and spelling.	Sentence structure is excellent, contributing to the effectiveness of the writing with almost no errors in grammar, mechanics, and spelling.	Sentence structure is good, contributing somewhat to the effectiveness of the writing with few errors in grammar, mechanics, and spelling.	Sentence structure is acceptable with some errors in grammar, mechanics, and spelling.	Sentence structure does not contribute to the effectiveness of the writing, and there are many errors in grammar, mechanics, and spelling.
Self-Reflection	Self-reflection is written effectively with references to texts read during this unit and shows understanding of the topics as they relate to current social issues.	Self-reflection is written well with references to texts read during this unit and shows understanding of the topics as they relate to current social issues.	Self-reflection is written somewhat effectively with some references to texts read during this unit, but current social issues may not be addressed effectively.	Self-reflection is not written well; the topic is not discussed effectively with little references to texts read during this unit, and current social issues are not addressed effectively.	Self-reflection is written without any understanding of topics covered in class or how they relate to current social issues.
					_____ / 20

Civil Rights

LESSON 3.3 RUBRIC
Persuasive Essay

Civil Rights

	Exceeds Expectations 5 points	Proficient 4 points	Developed 3 points	Emerging 2 points	Novice 1 point
Organization	Introduction clearly states the position/claim; more than three reasons are included; supporting information is relevant, strongly connected to the topic, presented in a logical order; there is a counterargument and a strong conclusion.	Introduction states the position/claim; three reasons are included; most supporting information is connected to the topic, and presented in a clear, logical order; there is a counterargument and conclusion.	Introduction states the position/claim; two reasons are included; some supporting information is relevant, connected to the topic, and presented in a logical order; there is a counterargument and a conclusion.	Introduction states the position, but it is somewhat unclear; reasons are given, but they are weak; supporting information is somewhat connected to the topic but not always presented in a logical order; there is a weak conclusion.	Introduction is unclear; position is vague; reasons are not given; supporting information is not always relevant or presented in a logical order; there is no conclusion.
Transitions	Transitions are solid and connect paragraphs appropriately	Transitions are connected to paragraphs; however, there may be one statement inappropriately placed/not connected to the topic sentence.	Transitions are connected to paragraphs; however, the statements are vague and may not connect well to the topic sentence.	Transitions are not connected and are too vague to make a connection to topic sentences.	Transitions are nonexistent; paragraphs do not have any cohesion or logic.
Evidence of Research and Knowledge	Outstanding evidence of research and depth of content knowledge, with a wide variety of sources referenced.	Clear evidence of research and depth of content knowledge, with four sources referenced.	Evidence of research and some content knowledge, with three sources referenced.	Some evidence of research and little content knowledge, with two sources referenced.	No evidence of research and little to no content knowledge, with one or no sources referenced.
Sentence Structure, Grammar, Mechanics, and Spelling	Sentence structure is outstanding, greatly contributing to the effectiveness of the writing with no errors in grammar, mechanics, and spelling.	Sentence structure is excellent, contributing to the effectiveness of the writing with almost no errors in grammar, mechanics, and spelling.	Sentence structure is good, contributing somewhat to the effectiveness of the writing with few errors in grammar, mechanics, and spelling.	Sentence structure is acceptable with some errors in grammar, mechanics, and spelling.	Sentence structure does not contribute to the effectiveness of the writing, and there are many errors in grammar, mechanics, and spelling.
					_____ / 16

LESSON 3.4
Governing Principles

Common Core State Standards

- RI.7.1
- RI.7.3
- RI.7.6
- W.7.9

Materials

- Lesson 3.4 Literature Analysis Model
- Student copies of "The Four Freedoms" speech by Franklin D. Roosevelt
- Student copies of "The Economic Bill of Rights" speech by Franklin D. Roosevelt
- Student copies of the Preamble and the Fourteenth Amendment to the U.S. Constitution
- Teacher's resource: "FDR Biography" by FDR Presidential Library & Museum (https://fdrlibrary.org/fdr-biography)

Estimated Time

- 60 minutes

Objectives

In this lesson, students will:
- analyze elements of the U.S. Constitution and compare them to a speech by President Franklin D. Roosevelt.

Content

Students will connect to previous lessons concerning civil rights and the law by locating persuasive language in speeches given by Franklin D. Roosevelt in 1941 and 1944. Students will connect Roosevelt's explanation of freedoms to the Preamble and Fourteenth Amendment to the U.S. Constitution.

Prior Knowledge

Students will need to have experience locating modes of persuasion (logos, pathos, and ethos) in speeches and using supporting evidence to draw conclusions regarding an author's tone and overall message.

INSTRUCTIONAL SEQUENCE

1. Ask students about their knowledge of President Franklin D. Roosevelt. Share information about the former president as needed (see Materials list).
2. Have students read "The Four Freedoms" speech by Franklin D. Roosevelt. For an initial analysis of the speech, have students complete Lesson 3.4 Literature Analysis Model. (See pp. 3–4 for more information about using the Literature Analysis Model.)

Teacher's Note. "The Four Freedoms" speech was the 1941 State of the Union Address, 11 months before the attack on Pearl Harbor. Roosevelt detailed four freedoms–freedom of speech, worship, from want, and from fear–which he proposed that people "everywhere in the world" should have and enjoy.

3. Have students read the Preamble to the U.S. Constitution and reread the Fourteenth Amendment. Ask students to look at "The Four Freedoms" speech again and underline Roosevelt's use of persuasive language (logos, pathos, and ethos) and to put an asterisk next to the freedoms given to Americans found in both the Preamble and the Fourteenth Amendment.
4. Discuss students' findings. You may guide students to this quote from "The Four Freedoms" speech and ask their opinion regarding the use of persuasion:

   As a nation we may take pride in the fact that we are soft-hearted; but we cannot afford to be soft-headed. We must always be wary of those who with sounding brass and a tinkling cymbal preach the "ism" of appeasement. We must especially beware of that small group of selfish men who would clip the wings of the American eagle in order to feather their own nests.

5. Then, have students read Roosevelt's "The Economic Bill of Rights." For an initial analysis of the speech, have students complete Lesson 3.4 Literature Analysis Model. (See pp. 3–4 for more information about using the Literature Analysis Model.)

Teacher's Note. "The Economic Bill of Rights," also known as the "Second Bill of Rights," was part of Roosevelt's 1944 State of the Union Address. He proposed eight rights which he did not believe the U.S. Constitution and the Bill of Rights adequately covered.

6. Ask students to look at "The Economic Bill of Rights" again and to underline Roosevelt's use of persuasive language (logos, pathos, and ethos).
7. Discuss students' findings. Ask students to compare "The Economic Bill of Rights" to "The Four Freedoms" speech. Guiding questions may include:
   - How are the speeches different?

- Are there any similarities in the use of language within the speeches?
- Did the speaker's tone change over the years?
- What are the rights available to every American "regardless of station, race, or creed" as written in "The Economic Bill of Rights"?

Extension Activities

Students may:

- create two Amendments to the Constitution and explain why these changes are necessary for today; or
- read George W. Bush's "9/11 Address to the Nation" and create a Venn diagram comparing it to Roosevelt's "The Four Freedoms" speech, identifying the similarities and differences in the use of persuasive language (logos, pathos, and ethos) used by both presidents.

LESSON 3.4
Literature Analysis Model

Directions: Complete this Literature Analysis Model about the speech by Franklin Delano Roosevelt.

Civil Rights

	_____ Speech by Franklin Delano Roosevelt
Key Words	
Important Ideas	
Tone	
Mood	
Imagery	
Symbolism	
Structure of Writing	

Note. Adapted from *Exploring America in the 1950s* (p. 10) by M. Sandling & K. L. Chandler, 2014, Waco, TX: Prufrock Press. Copyright 2014 by Center for Gifted Education. Adapted with permission.

LESSON 3.5
Self-Reflection

Common Core State Standards

- RL.7.1
- RI.7.3
- RI.7.5
- RI.7.6
- W.7.4
- W.7.9
- SL.7.1c
- SL.7.1d
- L.7.5c

Materials

- Lesson 3.5 Poetry Analysis
- Lesson 3.5 Literature Analysis Model
- Student copies of "Let America Be America Again" by Langston Hughes
- Student copies of "I, Too, Sing America" Langston Hughes (optional)
- Student copies of "Spirit of Liberty" speech by Judge Billings Learned Hand
- Colored pencils (red and blue for each student)
- Video: "Langston Hughes: Mini Biography" (http://www.biography.com/people/langston-hughes-9346313/videos/langston-hughes-mini-biography-2174109638)

Estimated Time

- 180 minutes

Objectives

In this lesson, students will:
- analyze how an author organizes a text, including how the major sections contribute to the whole and to the development of the ideas.

Content

Students will read and analyze poems and the use of persuasive language in speeches. They will analyze texts for their thematic content and references to freedom.

Prior Knowledge

Students will need experience with online research, analyzing and interpreting poetry, locating persuasive language in speeches, and using supporting evidence in texts to draw conclusions regarding an author's purpose.

INSTRUCTIONAL SEQUENCE

1. Ask students to review what they know about the First and Fourteenth Amendments to the U.S. Constitution.

2. Introduce Langston Hughes, showing the video biography. Students should understand that Hughes was an African American poet and was a leader of the Harlem Renaissance movement in New York during the 1920s.

3. Distribute "Let America Be America Again" by Langston Hughes. Hughes wrote the poem in 1935. Read the poem aloud to the class, as students look for shifts in the author's tone between anger (red) and positivity (blue) using their colored pencils. Encourage students to think of tone, central theme, and an extended metaphor. (The use of "dream" and its connection to civil rights is an extended metaphor.) Guiding questions may include:

   - In parentheses, Hughes states, "America was never America to me/There's never been equality for me." Based on the time period of this poem, what makes these statements so significant to the poem's content? What feeling is portrayed? Why?

   - Why does Hughes use a repetition of "I am" in the last three stanzas of the poem? What is he trying to convey to his audience?

   - What could be interpreted as the "American Dream" according to the poem?

> **Teacher's Note.** "I, Too, Sing America" can be used in place of "Let America Be America Again." However, "Let America Be America Again" has content that will work better with the speech studied in this lesson.

4. Divide students into groups of four and distribute Lesson 3.5 Poetry Analysis. Consider having students recreate this handout on chart paper to complete using markers and colored pencils. This could be used as a form of presentation or gallery walk if you choose. Discuss students' responses.

5. Introduce Judge Billings Learned Hand, who was a U.S. judge and judicial philosopher. He gave the "Spirit of Liberty" speech during World War II. Consider having students briefly research Learned Hand's occupation and philosophies.

6. Then, have students read the "Spirit of Liberty" speech by Learned Hand. For an initial analysis of the speech, have students complete Lesson 3.5 Literature Analysis Model. (See pp. 3–4 for more information about using the Literature Analysis Model.)

7. Discuss the speech, focusing on the following excerpt:

> I often wonder whether we do not rest our hopes too much upon constitutions, upon laws and upon courts. These are false hopes; believe me, these are false hopes. Liberty lies in the hearts of men and women; when it dies there, no constitution, no law, no court can even do much to help it. While it lies there it needs no constitution, no law, no court to save it. And what is this liberty which must lie in the hearts of men and women? It is not the ruthless, the unbridled will; it is not freedom to do as one likes. That is the denial of liberty, and leads straight to its overthrow.

Guiding questions may include:
- What makes the first line of the quote ironic?
- How does this quote resemble the ideals discussed in Hughes's poem?
- What are Hand's thoughts on civil liberties for all?

Extension Activities

Students may:
- write a response to Langston Hughes's "Let America Be America Again" from the perspective of Dr. Martin Luther King, Jr. (What would King say to Hughes? Would he agree with Hughes' perspective? Disagree? Would he be impartial?); or
- write a dialogue between Judge Learned Hand and Franklin D. Roosevelt (What will they discuss? How does Roosevelt react to Hand's thoughts on liberty?).

LESSON 3.5
Poetry Analysis

Directions: Read Langston Hughes's poem "Let America Be America Again" and complete the following chart.

Theme and Content	Response	Textual Evidence (Include Stanza)
What is the author's overall theme?		
What is the author's tone?		
Identify two types of literary devices used in the poem.		
What types of imagery are found in the poem?		
What is the moral of the poem?		
Do you believe that Dr. Martin Luther King, Jr. would agree with Langston Hughes's views? Why or why not?		

LESSON 3.5
Literature Analysis Model

Directions: Complete this Literature Analysis Model about the "Spirit of Liberty" speech by Judge Learned Hand.

"Spirit of Liberty" Speech by Judge Learned Hand	
Key Words	
Important Ideas	
Tone	
Mood	
Imagery	
Symbolism	
Structure of Writing	

Note. Adapted from *Exploring America in the 1950s* (p. 10) by M. Sandling & K. L. Chandler, 2014, Waco, TX: Prufrock Press. Copyright 2014 by Center for Gifted Education. Adapted with permission.

UNIT III
Culminating Essay Prompt

Directions: In this unit, you learned about civil rights in the U.S. and in South Africa and the use of persuasive language in speeches and poetry. Create your own speech about what you would like to change in society or within your community. Make sure the speech is persuasive and applies to the logic, emotional, or ethical (logos, pathos, or ethos) part of human nature.

UNIT IV

Tolerance

This unit centers on the theme of tolerance and how intolerance toward ideas and other cultures or races can lead to stereotyping, propaganda, and governmental control. Within the unit, students will read, analyze, evaluate, and interpret novels, poems, and nonfiction texts by authors such as Ray Bradbury, Nikki Giovanni, and Markus Zusak. Students will explore elements of persuasive language and the survival of the human spirit in the face of intolerance and control. Students will demonstrate their growing understanding of this theme through various projects, discussions, and persuasive writing.

LESSON 4.1

Censorship

Common Core State Standards

- RL.7.1
- RL.7.2
- RL.7.6
- W.7.7
- SL.7.1b
- SL.7.1c

Materials

- Lesson 4.1 Literature Analysis Model
- Lesson 4.1 Censorship Concept Organizer
- Lesson 4.1 Dystopian Society Concept Organizer
- Lesson 4.1 Understanding the Text
- Student copies of *Fahrenheit 451* by Ray Bradbury
- Student copies of "A Poem for My Librarian, Mrs. Long" by Nikki Giovanni

Estimated Time

- 120 minutes

Objectives

In this lesson, students will:
- understand and analyze an author's purpose and tone; and
- cite textual evidence in order to demonstrate understanding of what the text says explicitly as well as inferences drawn from the text.

Content

Students will read a poem and discern its meaning and connections to themes of tolerance and social and emotional freedom found in the novel *Fahrenheit 451* by Ray Bradbury. Students will study censorship and identify characteristics of dystopian societies. Then, students will write a constructed response.

Prior Knowledge

Students need to have read *Fahrenheit 451* by Ray Bradbury. Students will need some knowledge of the terms *censorship* and *dystopian*. Students should have experience using a close reading strategy, annotating, drawing conclusions based on an author's purpose, and rereading key passages for understanding. Students need to understand various types of figurative language, including assonance, consonance, rhyme scheme, and imagery.

INSTRUCTIONAL SEQUENCE

1. Have students read "A Poem for My Librarian, Mrs. Long" by Nikki Giovanni.
2. For an initial analysis of the poem, have students complete Lesson 4.1 Literature Analysis Model. (See pp. 3–4 for more information about using the Literature Analysis Model.) Have students pay attention to the treatment of African Americans in the South.
3. Ask students what they know about *censorship* and *dystopian societies* from their reading of "A Poem for My Librarian, Mrs. Long" by Nikki Giovanni and *Fahrenheit 451* by Ray Bradbury. Guiding questions may include:
   - Do you believe censorship is necessary?
   - Which types of items are censored today? Why? (Movies, video games, music, etc.)
   - Do you feel censored as a teenager in today's society? Why?
   - Do we have a perfect or imperfect society? Why?
   - What keeps everyone and everything in order within our society? How? (Laws, morals, etc.)
   - Can you identify any books or movies where a dystopian society was depicted? What were the characteristics of a dystopian society found in the book/movie? How did the characters react to their societies?

4. Distribute Lesson 4.1 Censorship Concept Organizer and Lesson 4.1 Dystopian Society Concept Organizer, explaining that they will use the handouts to explore the meanings of *censorship* and *dystopian society*. Model how to complete the organizer using a think-aloud strategy. Discuss students' findings as a class.
5. Discuss *Fahrenheit 451*, focusing on character connections, motifs, and figurative language. Guiding questions may include:
   - Why does Granger suggest that certain philosophers are worthy of preservation?
   - What does the use of the mechanical hound symbolize, and what does its reaction to Montag symbolize?
   - How does the burning of the books and the old woman connect to Montag's life?
   - How is this society controlled? Who controls the society and with what?
   - How is propaganda used to control the citizens?
   - What is the citizens' biggest fear? What do they perceive as the truth?

6. Distribute Lesson 4.1 Understanding the Text. Allow students to complete the chart with a partner. Discuss students' responses.
7. Then, have students write a short constructed response to one of the following prompts:
   - Montag meets Clarisse McClellan during Part I. Explain why Clarisse may be a symbol of enlightenment or dramatic change for Montag. Use examples from the text to support your response.
   - In Part II, Montag speaks to Faber regarding his feelings and the burning books. He says, "Nobody listens anymore. I can't talk to the walls because they're yelling at me. I can't talk to my wife; she listens to the walls. I just want someone to hear what I have to say. And maybe if I talk long enough, it'll make sense. And I want you to teach me

to understand what I read." In your own words, interpret Montag's thoughts. Also, why would Montag believe Faber would be sympathetic to his plight? Use textual evidence.

- What is the significance of using "noise" as a motif in the text? How does this motif connect to the novel's theme? Use textual evidence.
- Explain how Ray Bradbury, conveys to readers that one's individuality and cultural identity has been "burned" through conformity and censorship. Use textual evidence.

Extension Activities

Students may:

- research a list of banned books from the year 1980 and, in a short persuasive essay, discuss why the books were banned and why they should not be banned today;
- watch the 1966 version of the film *Fahrenheit 451* and compare and contrast it to the text in a Venn diagram, paying attention to characters' actions, mood, tone, and variations between the text and film; or
- research the book burnings conducted by the German Student Association in Nazi Germany and Austria in the 1930s and, in a compare and contrast essay, compare the actions and reasons for burning the books to those found in *Fahrenheit 451*.

LESSON 4.1
Literature Analysis Model

Directions: Complete this Literature Analysis Model about "A Poem for My Librarian, Mrs. Long" by Nikki Giovanni.

"A Poem for My Librarian, Mrs. Long" by Nikki Giovanni	
Key Words	
Important Ideas	
Tone	
Mood	
Imagery	
Symbolism	
Structure of Writing	

Note. Adapted from *Exploring America in the 1950s* (p. 10) by M. Sandling & K. L. Chandler, 2014, Waco, TX: Prufrock Press. Copyright 2014 by Center for Gifted Education. Adapted with permission.

LESSON 4.1
Censorship Concept Organizer

Directions: Complete each of the boxes based on the term *censorship*.

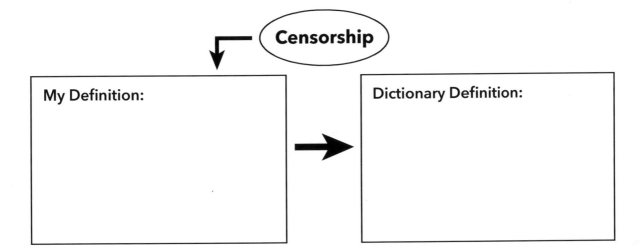

Tolerance

My Definition:

Dictionary Definition:

Your Ideas About Censorship:

Example:

Nonexample:

Censorship In Our Society:

Related Words/Phrases:

A Sentence Using the Word *Censorship*:

LESSON 4.1

Dystopian Society Concept Organizer

Directions: Complete each of the boxes based on the term *dystopian society*.

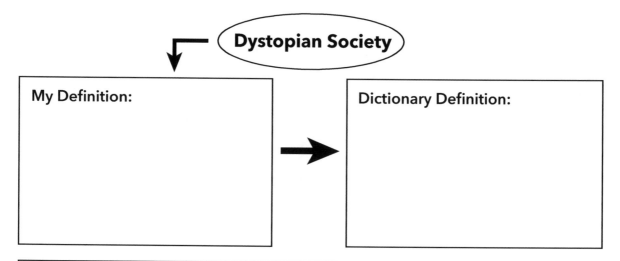

Dystopian Society

My Definition:

Dictionary Definition:

Your Ideas About Dystopian Society:

Example:	Books or Short Stories About Dystopian Society:	Related Words/Phrases:
Nonexample:		

A Sentence Using the Phrase *Dystopian Society*:

Tolerance

LESSON 4.1
Understanding the Text

Directions: Answer the questions about *Fahrenheit 451* by Ray Bradbury with textual evidence.

Understanding the Text	Response	Textual Evidence
What does the title of the novel symbolize?		
Choose one type of literary device, such as symbolism, imagery, or metaphor, and explain its significance to the novel or character(s).		
What examples of conflict are shown in the novel? Choose two types of conflict, such as man vs. man, man vs. himself, man vs. nature, or man vs. society. Explain their significance to the main character's situation.		
What is the overall theme?		

Tolerance

Understanding the Text	Response	Textual Evidence
Which type of characterization, direct or indirect, can be found within the novel, and how does the selected characterization contribute to the understanding of the novel's theme?		
What is the significance of books, according to Beatty?		
Think about Montag and Mildred's relationship and Montag's friendship with Clarisse. How are Clarisse and Mildred different? Describe the differences in the two relationships.		
Think of the characteristics of the "television wall." Do we have a version of a "television wall" within our society?		
Describe the characteristic attributes of Montag, Faber, and Beatty with regard to books, magazines, and/or newspapers. What do they say? How do they act? What do they look like? What are their feelings?		

LESSON 4.2
Don't Judge Me

Common Core State Standards

- RL.7.1
- RL.7.2
- W.7.2
- SL.7.1b
- SL.7.1c

Materials

- Lesson 4.2 Tolerance Concept Organizer
- Lesson 4.2 Literature Analysis Model
- Lesson 4.2 Speech Venn Diagram
- Lesson 4.2 Rubric: Persuasive Essay
- Student copies of "Tolerance" by E. M. Forster
- Student copies of excerpts from *Fahrenheit 451* by Ray Bradbury (Part I, Section II, Captain Beatty's speech to Montag; Part III, Section III, Granger's speech about his grandfather)
- Student copies of *The Book Thief* by Markus Zusak

Estimated Time

- 150 minutes

Objectives

In this lesson, students will:
- understand an author's purpose, tone, and use of persuasive language within a text.

Content

Students will continue to explore censorship, connecting to how a lack of tolerance can lead to stereotypes and governmental control, as discussed in an essay by E. M. Forster. Students will also revisit parts of *Fahrenheit 451* that relate to tolerance and how some people within the society were not tolerant of others' knowledge or viewpoints. Then, students will write a persuasive essay on a selected topic.

Prior Knowledge

Students will need to have experience with shared-inquiry discussions and writing persuasive essays using supporting evidence to draw conclusions in reference to an author's purpose and textual themes after reading. Outside of class, students will need to begin reading *The Book Thief* by Markus Zusak in preparation for Lesson 4.4.

INSTRUCTIONAL SEQUENCE

1. Ask students for their definition of the term *tolerance*. Guiding questions may include:
   - If you are in a movie theatre, name a few behaviors you must tolerate as you watch the film (e.g., coughing, sneezing, talking, chewing loudly, snacks rustling).
   - Think of a time when you were in a lunch or grocery line. What did you tolerate as you stood there?
   - Give an example of something you tolerate every day.

2. Distribute Lesson 4.2 Tolerance Concept Organizer, explaining that students will use the handout to explore their meaning and the actual meaning of *tolerance*. Model how to complete the organizer using a think-aloud strategy. Discuss students' findings as a class.

3. Have students read "Tolerance" by E. M. Forster. "Tolerance" is a brief essay written during the World War II era. In the essay, Forster discusses how tolerance of one another is necessary for reconstruction and that false love, prejudice, and stereotyping have no place in building a flourishing civilization.

4. For an initial analysis of the essay, have students complete Lesson 4.2 Literature Analysis Model. (See pp. 3–4 for more information about using the Literature Analysis Model.) Guiding questions may include:
   - What does it mean to have a sound state of mind?
   - What does Forster mean when he says that tolerance is a very dull virtue?
   - What is the overall theme of the essay?

5. Have students create 3–5 questions to begin a shared-inquiry discussion. Students' questions should focus on allusion, the author's purpose, tolerance, and persuasive language. Guiding questions may include:
   - Which biblical allusions do you recognize and what is their significance to the essay's theme?
   - This essay was written during World War II; explain World War II's influence on the writer's purpose.
   - Which type of persuasive language did the author use? Pathos, logos, or ethos? Give examples from the text.
   - How does Forster compare "love" to "tolerance"?

Teacher's Note. A shared-inquiry discussion allows students to agree or disagree with each other using text-based responses and build upon the responses with new questions. Students listen and respond, and the group leader (teacher) asks questions based on the direction of the discussion. Every student must answer at least once with a complete response using evidence from the text.

6. After the discussion, have students reread Beatty's and Granger's speeches from *Fahrenheit 451* (see Materials list). Distribute Lesson 4.2 Speech Venn Diagram, which will serve as a brainstorming activity before students write a persuasive essay.

7. Share with students that they will write a persuasive essay, responding to the following prompt:

    In a five-paragraph essay, write a persuasive essay answering the question: Do you believe there is a lack of tolerance in today's society? Are people able to freely express their own cultural, political, and social diversity? Research a real-life event using your local newspaper or national news where someone's cultural, political, or social rights were violated and intolerance was shown. Use this additional information within your essay.

8. Distribute Lesson 4.2 Rubric: Persuasive Essay before students begin.

Extension Activities

Students may:
- watch Coach Boone's speech in *Remember the Titans* (available on YouTube) and generate a short constructed response, answering the following prompt:

    Forster said that sometimes people dislike others simply because of how they look, what they do, how they smell, etc. A person's dislike of another has nothing to do with the person, but that which is superficial. Think about this comment and Coach Boone's speech in *Remember the Titans* when he says, "You don't have to like each other, but you will respect each other." How do these words relate to the overall themes shared in Forster's essay and *Fahrenheit 451*?

LESSON 4.2
Tolerance Concept Organizer

Directions: Complete each of the boxes based on the term *tolerance*.

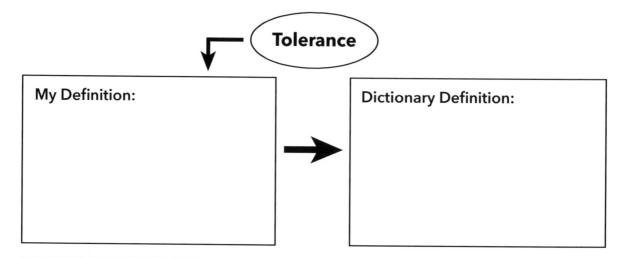

Tolerance

My Definition:		Dictionary Definition:

Your Ideas About Tolerance:

Example:	Places and/or Ways You Have Shown Tolerance to Others:	Related Words/Phrases:
Nonexample:		

A Sentence Using the Word *Tolerance*:

Tolerance

LESSON 4.2
Literature Analysis Model

Directions: Complete this Literature Analysis Model about "Tolerance" by E. M. Forster.

"Tolerance" by E. M. Forster	
Key Words	
Important Ideas	
Tone	
Mood	
Imagery	
Symbolism	
Structure of Writing	

Tolerance

Note. Adapted from *Exploring America in the 1950s* (p. 10) by M. Sandling & K. L. Chandler, 2014, Waco, TX: Prufrock Press. Copyright 2014 by Center for Gifted Education. Adapted with permission.

LESSON 4.2
Speech Venn Diagram

Directions: Read each speech and the essay and determine similarities and differences between the three in reference to conformity. Fill in your responses within the diagram.

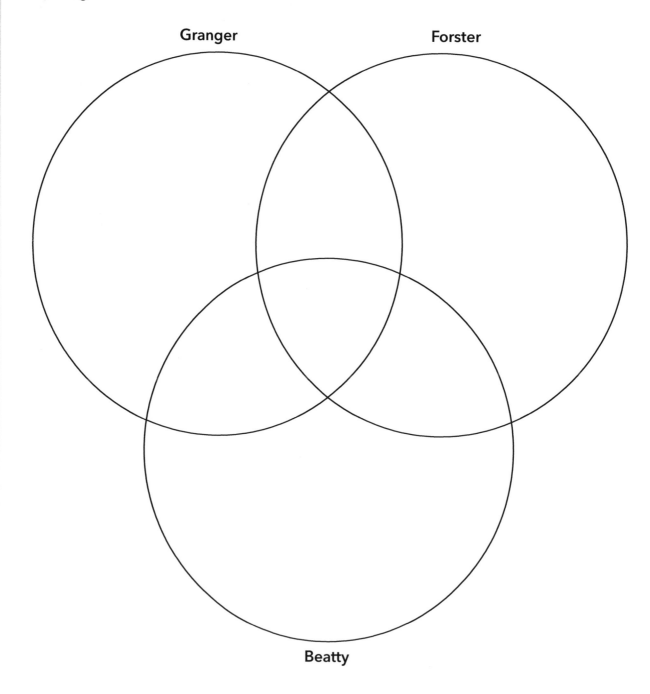

Tolerance

LESSON 4.2 RUBRIC
Persuasive Essay

	Exceeds Expectations 5 points	Proficient 4 points	Developed 3 points	Emerging 2 points	Novice 1 point
Organization	Introduction clearly states the position/claim; more than three reasons are included; supporting information is relevant, strongly connected to the topic, presented in a logical order; there is a counterargument and a strong conclusion.	Introduction states the position/claim; three reasons are included; most supporting information is connected to the topic, and presented in a clear, logical order; there is a counterargument and conclusion.	Introduction states the position/claim; two reasons are included; some supporting information is relevant, connected to the topic, and presented in a logical order; there is a counterargument and a conclusion.	Introduction states the position, but it is somewhat unclear; reasons are given, but they are weak; supporting information is somewhat connected to the topic but not always presented in a logical order; there is a weak conclusion.	Introduction is unclear; position is vague; reasons are not given; supporting information is not always relevant or presented in a logical order; there is no conclusion.
Transitions	Transitions are solid and connect paragraphs appropriately	Transitions are connected to paragraphs; however, there may be one statement inappropriately placed/not connected to the topic sentence.	Transitions are connected to paragraphs; however, the statements are vague and may not connect well to the topic sentence.	Transitions are not connected and are too vague to make a connection to topic sentences.	Transitions are nonexistent; paragraphs do not have any cohesion or logic.
Evidence of Research and Knowledge	Outstanding evidence of research and depth of content knowledge, with a wide variety of sources referenced.	Clear evidence of research and depth of content knowledge, with four sources referenced.	Evidence of research and some content knowledge, with three sources referenced.	Some evidence of research and little content knowledge, with two sources referenced.	No evidence of research and little to no content knowledge, with one or no sources referenced.
Sentence Structure, Grammar, Mechanics, and Spelling	Sentence structure is outstanding, greatly contributing to the effectiveness of the writing with no errors in grammar, mechanics, and spelling.	Sentence structure is excellent, contributing to the effectiveness of the writing with almost no errors in grammar, mechanics, and spelling.	Sentence structure is good, contributing somewhat to the effectiveness of the writing with few errors in grammar, mechanics, and spelling.	Sentence structure is acceptable with some errors in grammar, mechanics, and spelling.	Sentence structure does not contribute to the effectiveness of the writing, and there are many errors in grammar, mechanics, and spelling.
					_____ / 16

Tolerance

LESSON 4.3

You Say It, I Believe It

Common Core State Standards

- RL.7.1
- RL.7.2
- RL.7.6
- W.7.7
- SL.7.1b
- SL.7.1c

Materials

- Lesson 4.3 Propaganda Concept Organizer
- Lesson 4.3 Artwork Analysis
- Student copies of *The Book Thief* by Markus Zusak
- Examples of persuasive commercials, such as:
  - "Nicole Randall in Propel Fitness Water Commercial" (https://www.youtube.com/watch?v=pgOw9HfzDXc)
  - "Propel Zero–Drops of Life" (https://www.youtube.com/watch?v=O7ZfAqtv08g)
  - "ETRADE Top 5 Baby Commercials" (https://youtube.com/watch?v=hashPaU7Dpk)
  - "Coca Cola: Dragon Fireworks" (https://youtube.com/watch?v=_yX6VnY05Eo)

- Examples of World War II propaganda posters, such as:
  - "Four Freedoms" (http://www.archives.gov/exhibits/powers_of_persuasion/four_freedoms/four_freedoms.html)
  - "This Is Nazi Brutality" (http://www.archives.gov/exhibits/powers_of_persuasion/this_is_nazi_brutality/this_is_nazi_brutality.html)
  - "Stamp 'Em Out!" (http://www.archives.gov/exhibits/powers_of_persuasion/stamp_em_out/stamp_em_out.html)

- Artwork by Auschwitz Survivor Jan Komski, such as:
  - *Eating and Starvation* (http://remember.org/komski/komski-paintings1-001)
  - *A Photo for the Album* (http://remember.org/komski/komski-drawings1-001)

- Teacher's resource: "Nazi Propaganda and Censorship" by the United States Holocaust and Memorial Museum (https://www.ushmm.org/outreach/en/article.php?ModuleId=10007677)

Estimated Time

- 120 minutes

147

Objectives

In this lesson, students will:
- understand the use of persuasive language and opinion in propaganda.

Content

Students will discuss persuasive language and how its use can coax society into emotions, bargains, and illusions of perfection. Students will study propaganda used during World War II to further understand the power of persuasion and uses of symbolism, imagery, and loaded language.

Prior Knowledge

Students will need to have read through at least Part II of *The Book Thief* by Markus Zusak. Students should have some knowledge of World War II. They should be able to analyze an author's message and persuasive language (logos, pathos, ethos) in text and other media.

INSTRUCTIONAL SEQUENCE

1. Ask students: *What is the purpose of advertisements? Why do we listen to, watch, or read them?* Students should recognize that advertisements assist in purchasing goods and services. Persuasive language can influence emotions or reasoning, which may promote buying or belief in false truths.

2. View selected persuasive television advertisements (see Materials list). Guiding questions may include:
   - What is the underlying message?
   - Who is the audience? What is the focused age group? How do you know?
   - Which kind of persuasive language is used (logos, pathos, or ethos)?
   - Which elements are used to make you want to *buy* the product?

3. Tell students that a more powerful form of advertising is *propaganda*. Distribute Lesson 4.3 Propaganda Concept Organizer for students to complete. Discuss students' responses.

4. Then, tell students that propaganda was used during World War II, the time period of *The Book Thief* by Markus Zusak. Show students examples of propaganda posters from World War II (see Materials list). As you show the posters, ask students which category of propaganda would fit the poster appropriately and why (see Teacher's Note). Write their responses on the board. Other guiding questions may include:
   - How do the pictures influence the public's emotions?
   - What do you notice about the colors?
   - How are the Germans and Japanese displayed in the posters?

5. Share with students some of the ways in which the Nazis used propaganda and censorship (see Materials list). Ask students how they would feel if they were subjected to similar censorship.

> ***Teacher's Note.*** Share with students that there are seven types of propaganda according to *The Fine Art of Propaganda*:
> - **Transfer:** Carrying of authority;
> - **Plain Folks:** My ideas are just like yours;
> - **Bandwagon:** Everyone does the same thing;
> - **Glittering Generality:** Wholesome virtue;
> - **Testimonial:** Someone giving a stamp of approval;
> - **Name-Calling:** Bad labeling;
> - **Card Stacking:** Use of facts, false statements, or distractions. (Lee & Lee, 1939, 22-23)
>
> Write these terms on the board with a brief definition of each.

6. With the knowledge students have acquired in this lesson and their reading of *The Book Thief* so far, begin a brief discussion. Guiding questions may include:
   - How was propaganda used during World War II?
   - Why was propaganda so important to the war effort?
   - How did propaganda display a lack of tolerance?

7. Introduce students to Jan Komski, an artist and Auschwitz survivor. Display the painting *Eating and Starvation* or the drawing *A Photo for the Album*. Distribute Lesson 4.3 Artwork Analysis. Instruct students to complete the activity based on the pamphlet excerpt, propaganda poster(s), and artwork. Discuss students' responses.

Extension Activities

Students may:
- research the Nuremburg Laws of Germany and the pass laws of South Africa, and use a Venn diagram to document their differences and similarities; or
- write a poem from the perspective of Jan Komski about his detainment in Auschwitz, using one of his paintings or drawing as inspiration.

LESSON 4.3
Propaganda Concept Organizer

Directions: Complete each of the boxes based on the term *propaganda*.

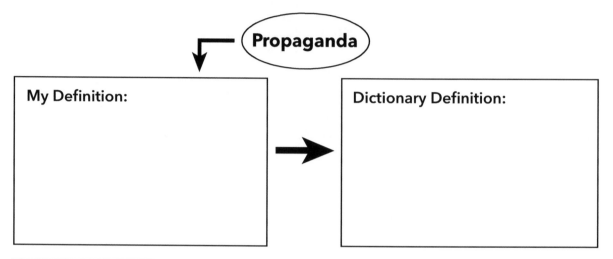

Your Ideas About Propaganda:

Example:	A Propaganda Drawing for Something You Would Like to Change:	Related Words/Phrases:
Nonexample:		

A Sentence Using the Word *Propaganda*:

Tolerance

LESSON 4.3
Artwork Analysis

Directions: Complete the questions below using the artwork and other materials you have viewed during this lesson. Prepare to share with the class.

1. Describe Jan Komski's artwork with complete sentences.

2. What is happening in the artwork? Use evidence from the work.

3. What colors or lighting is used? Why?

4. Which season of the year is depicted? Use evidence from the work.

Tolerance

5. Discuss the differences between the visual elements of Komski's artwork and the American war posters.

6. Did the artwork by Komski evoke emotion in you as the viewer? Explain with evidence.

7. How were Nazi book burnings of Jewish and non-Jewish books an example of intolerance?

8. According to the article, what was the massive propaganda campaign begun by the Germans during 1933?

LESSON 4.4
The Rescuer

Common Core State Standards

- RL.7.1
- RL.7.2
- RL.7.6
- W.7.7
- SL.7.1b
- SL.7.1c

Materials

- Lesson 4.4 Literature Analysis Model
- Lesson 4.4 Understanding the Text
- Lesson 4.4 Character Tracking
- Lesson 4.4 Discussion Strategy
- Lesson 4.4 Peer Evaluation
- Student copies of *The Book Thief* by Markus Zusak
- Video: "Adolf Hitler: Mini Biography" (http://www.biography.com/people/adolf-hitler-9340144/videos/adolf-hitler-mini-biography-2232485039)
- Index cards (3–5 per student)

Estimated Time

- 120 minutes

Objectives

In this lesson, students will:
- compare and contrast a fictional portrayal of a time, place, or character and a historical account of the same period to understand how authors of fiction use or alter history.

Content

Students will learn about World War II and Adolf Hitler. They will continue to analyze *The Book Thief* by Markus Zusak.

Prior Knowledge

Students will need to have read *The Book Thief* by Markus Zusak. Students will need experience using supporting evidence and textual details to draw conclusions. Students should understand how to conduct a discussion with their peers and to read texts with a purpose of recognizing characters' characteristics, theme, author's purpose, and conflict.

INSTRUCTIONAL SEQUENCE

1. Have students analyze at least one chapter *The Book Thief* by Markus Zusak using the Literature Analysis Model. For an initial analysis of the novel, work with students to complete Lesson 4.4 Literature Analysis Model. You may wish to leave some of the boxes blank that may not be particularly relevant for this type of text. (See pp. 3–4 for more information about using the Literature Analysis Model.)

2. Ask students what they know about Adolf Hitler and his role in World War II. Show Hitler's biography video. Guiding questions may include:
   - How did Hitler gain support for his cause of preserving the "supreme race" through the use of propaganda?
   - How do Hitler's actions connect to the theme of tolerance?
   - How does Hitler's role in history and his intolerance of others connect to what you read in *The Book Thief*?

3. Distribute Lesson 4.4 Character Tracking, where students will record major characters, their challenges, and resolutions to those challenges.

4. Then, divide students in to groups of 2–3 and distribute Lesson 4.4 Understanding the Text. Advise them to work together and discuss the handout.

5. Distribute 3–5 index cards to each student. Have students create 3–5 questions about the novel in preparation for a fishbowl discussion. Encourage students to question the text by asking themselves probing questions about the characters' actions, emotions, theme, author's purpose, conflict, vocabulary, and types of conflict found within the text, for example:
   - Explain the relationship between Liesel and Hans. What do they have in common? Why is it important?
   - Why is the "power of words" important in this novel?
   - How is intolerance displayed in this novel through the actions or speech of others?
   - Death is personified, and he is in conflict with war. Why is war so intolerable?

6. Have students record each of their questions on an index card and place them in a box.

7. Allow students to draw one or two questions from the box and sit in a fishbowl circle—some students seated in an inner circle and some in an outer circle—for discussion. Have each student in the inner circle partner with a student in the outer circle. Outer circle students will track the discussion on Lesson 4.4 Discussion Strategy and then rate their partner's performance with Lesson 4.4 Peer Evaluation.

Teacher's Note. During the fishbowl discussion, allow students in the inner circle to read a selected question and one member within the circle may answer at a time. Others in the circle may add additional information to the response, but they must remember to show discussion etiquette of not talking over one another and showing respect for other's ideas and opinions. Students placed in the outer circle are to watch, listen, and document. Outer circle students should have one member assigned to them so they may track the discussion.

8. Then, have students in the inner and outer circles switch to conclude the discussion.

Extension Activities

Students may:

- identify examples of the three types of irony (dramatic, verbal, and situational) found in *The Book Thief* and write a brief essay about how one or all three may have assisted in shaping the character of Liesel Meminger;
- identify the various literary devices found within the novel and write a brief essay about how those devices may influence the overall theme; or
- write a new ending to Liesel's story from Death's point of view.

LESSON 4.4
Literature Analysis Model

Directions: Complete this Literature Analysis Model about a chapter from *The Book Thief* by Markus Zusak.

Tolerance

	The Book Thief: Chapter _____
Key Words	
Important Ideas	
Tone	
Mood	
Imagery	
Symbolism	
Structure of Writing	

Note. Adapted from *Exploring America in the 1950s* (p. 10) by M. Sandling & K. L. Chandler, 2014, Waco, TX: Prufrock Press. Copyright 2014 by Center for Gifted Education. Adapted with permission.

LESSON 4.4
Character Tracking

Directions: Complete the following chart regarding the main characters in *The Book Thief*.

Character	Challenge	Resolution
Liesel Meminger		

Tolerance

LESSON 4.4
Understanding the Text

Directions: After reading *The Book Thief,* complete the following chart. Use textual evidence for support.

Understanding the Text	Response	Textual Evidence
What does the title of the novel symbolize?		
Choose one type of literary device, such as symbolism, imagery, or dialogue and explain its significance to the story's character(s). Explain the importance of Death as the narrator of this novel.		
Which examples of conflict are shown in this novel? Choose two types of conflict, such as man vs. man, man vs. himself, man vs. nature, or man vs. society. Explain their significance to the main character's situation.		
What is the overall theme of the novel?		
Which type of characterization, direct or indirect, can be found in the novel, and how does the selected characterization contribute to the understanding of the novel's theme?		

Tolerance

LESSON 4.4
Discussion Strategy

Directions: Observe and record you partner's contributions to the discussion in the inner circle. When your partner answers a question, record his or her response and write down your response to your partner's answer, noting whether you agree or disagree.

Partner's Name: _____

Main Idea of the Discussion and Partner's Response	Personal Response Regarding the Discussion
Example Question: *In the Prologue, Death uses a mixture of colors, what may one infer regarding the use of colors to identify individuals?* **Partner's Response:** *I think . . . because . . . and in the text . . .*	**My Response:** *I agree/disagree because . . .*

Tolerance

LESSON 4.3
Peer Evaluation

Directions: After the discussion, evaluate your partner's participation. Choose a rating of 1–5, with 1 as the lowest score. Give comments if necessary.

Partner's Name: _____

Details	Rating	Comments
Asked a question pertaining to the text or characters found within the text.	5 4 3 2 1	
Answered questions effectively using textual evidence.	5 4 3 2 1	
Utilized an effective rebuttal to an opposing opinion.	5 4 3 2 1	
Maintained discussion etiquette. He or she did not talk over anyone else and waited until the other person finished before responding.	5 4 3 2 1	

Tolerance

UNIT IV
Culminating Essay Prompt

Directions: In this unit, you have read two novels regarding the plight of the human spirit and how intolerance may lead to stereotypes and prejudices in society. You have understood how the use of persuasive language and propaganda can twist the truth into someone else's reality. Now it is time to share your story. Write an expository essay detailing why it is important to show humanity, respect, and tolerance of others and their ideas. Use examples from any of the texts or media you have viewed to support your response.

Tolerance

ANSWER KEY

Lesson 1.1 Poetry Analysis

Sample answers are in bold.

Title of Poem: **"A Minor Bird"**		
Type of Conflict: **Man versus nature**		
Theme and Content	**Response**	**Textual Evidence (Include Line Numbers)**
What is the theme of the selection?	**The inability to appreciate nature**	**"I have wished a bird would fly away" (Line 1)**
What is the author's tone in this poem?	**Angry, depressed, sad**	**"I have wished . . ." (Line 1); "Have clapped . . ." (Line 3); "When it seemed . . ." (Line 4)**
Identify two types of figurative language used in this poem.	**Imagery, alliteration. (Others may include symbolism and onomatopoeia.)**	**Clapped hands (Line 3); bird, blame (Line 6); silence, song (Line 8)**
Are smell, sight, touch, taste, or sound implied in the poem? How?	**Yes; through the use of onomatopoeia.**	**"Clapped" (Line 3)**
What is the poem's rhyme scheme?	**AABBCCDD**	**Lines 1–8**
Generate one discussion question that you and your partner will share with another group.	**Answers will vary.**	

Lesson 1.2 Understanding the Text

Sample answers are in bold.

Title and Author: **"The Treasure of Lemon Brown" by Walter Dean Myers**		
Understanding the Text	**Response**	**Textual Evidence**
What does the title of the short story symbolize?	**Answers will vary.**	**Answers will vary.**

Understanding the Text	Response	Textual Evidence
Choose one type of literary device, such as symbolism, imagery, or dialogue, and explain its significance to the story's character(s).	**Symbolism: The clippings and harmonica are a connection to Lemon Brown's past and shaped his personality. They continued to give him hope and memories to live every day. These items were so precious to him that he was willing to lose his life over them.**	**"The old man carefully took off the plastic and unfolded it. He revealed some yellowed newspaper clippings and a battered harmonica."**
What examples of conflict are shown in this short story? Choose two types of conflict, such as man vs. man, man vs. himself, man vs. nature, or man vs. society. Explain their significance to the main character's situation.	**Man vs. self and man vs. man. Students may include that Greg's conflicts influenced him to leave home and find out who he truly was as a person and to appreciate his life.**	**Students may include the following evidence: report cards, father's speeches, or thugs in the building.**
What is the overall theme of the story?	**Coming of age**	**"Greg pushed the button over the bell marked Ridley, thought of the lecture he knew his father would give him, and smiled."**
Which type of characterization can be found in the short story? How does the selected characterization contribute to the understanding of the story's theme?	**Students may write about Greg's curiosity or Lemon Brown's idealistic qualities.**	

Lesson 1.3 Where Is John?

Sample answers are in bold.

Place	Translation	Conflict
Great Dead Places	**Homes; past**	**External—John feared the unknown.**
Place of the Gods	**New York; history**	**External—John finds various unknown items and he is curious about their functions; he begins to try/look/drink some of the items; external—John's father forbids him from traveling to the forbidden place; internal—John wants to see the forbidden place.**

Place	Translation	Conflict
Forest People	**Rivals of John's people; the primitive side of advancement**	**External—John thought his people were more advanced and that the primitiveness of the Forest People was a step backward for his kind.**
Old Writings	**Keys to the past**	**Internal—John wants to learn more of the past; he does not want to forget the old writings despite the fact that he does not understand them.**
Dead God	**Man**	**Internal—John wants to know how did he come to be and what does he have in common with the gods; internal—John discovers that gods were men who built things and destroyed them.**

Lesson 1.5 Conflict

Sample answers are in bold.

Dictionary Definition of Conflict: **Strong disagreement between people, groups, etc., that often results in angry argument; a difference that prevents agreement; disagreement.**	Group's Definition: **Answers will vary.**	
Question	**Answer**	**Textual Evidence**
What type of conflict is shown between Suyuan Woo and Jing-mei Woo? How is this conflict significant to the characters' development over the course of the story/novel?	**External; mother vs. daughter. Jing-mei defies her mother regarding the continuing of her piano lessons. Students may refer to Jing-mei wanting to be a prodigy until she realized the amount of work it involved, or that her mother was living a dream through her daughter. When Jing-mei speaks loudly against her mother, she begins her independence.**	**"'Then I wish I weren't your daughter, I wish you weren't my mother,' I shouted . . .";** **"'Then I wish I'd never been born!' I shouted. 'I wish I were dead! Like them.' . . . her face went blank, her mouth closed, her arms went slack, and she backed out of the room . . .";** **"I had new thoughts, willful thoughts . . ."**

Question	Answer	Textual Evidence
What type of conflict is shown between Lindo Jong and Waverly Jong? How is this conflict significant to the characters' development over the course of the story/novel?	**External; mother vs. daughter. Waverly does not want to be praised in public regarding her chess playing. At first it was fun and she enjoyed it, but it soon became a task. Waverly becomes strong in her ideas when she tells her mother how she truly feels about being displayed. This sets the stage for the character to speak up for what she wants.**	**"'Why do you have to use me to show off? If you want to show off, then why don't you learn to play chess?' My mother's eyes turned into dangerous black slits. She had no words for me, just sharp silence."**
Explain the generational conflict found between the daughters and the mothers. How did this conflict influence the daughters' decisions? Use textual evidence for support.	**The mothers came from China and the daughters grew up in America with some traditions and values instilled by their parents. Due to growing up in a different culture, the daughters begin to exhibit strong decision-making skills, which shape their futures in the novel.**	

Lesson 1.5 Symbolism

Sample answers are in bold.

Dictionary Definition of Symbolism: **Artistic imitation or invention that is a method of revealing or suggesting immaterial, ideal, or otherwise intangible truth or states.**	Group's Definition: **Answers will vary.**	
Question	**Answer**	**Textual Evidence**
In "Rules of the Game," what is the significance of the "wind" as Waverly played chess with her opponent?	**Students may focus on Waverly's feelings or her view of her opponent.**	**Answers will vary.**
In "Rules of the Game," interpret the following lines in your own words: "As I began to play, the boy disappeared, the color ran out of the room . . ."	**Answers will vary; students may interpret the quote as a way of escaping or a concentration strategy.**	**Answers will vary.**

Question	Answer	Textual Evidence
In "Two Kinds," what did the piano symbolize for Jing-mei? What did the piano symbolize for Jing-mei's mother?	**For Jing-mei, students may say the piano symbolizes work, forgiveness, or prodigy. For her mother, they may say it symbolizes living through her daughter, a way of healing their relationship, or pride.**	Answers will vary.
In "Two Kinds," what is the significance of the title of the piano piece, "Pleading Child"?	**Jing-mei pleaded with her mother to reconsider the piano lessons—she did not want them anymore. Her mother ignored her pleas.**	**Answers will vary.**
Interpret the following lines from "Two Kinds" in your own words: "And for the first time, or so it seemed, I noticed the piece on the right-hand side. It was called 'Perfectly Contented.' I tried to play this one as well. It had a lighter melody but with the same flowing rhythm and turned out to be quite easy. 'Pleading Child' was shorter but slower; 'Perfectly Contented' was longer but faster. And after I had played them both a few times, I realized they were two halves of the same song."	**Students' interpretations may include seeing the piano as a piece offering or trophy for hard work unnoticed; "Pleading Child" could represent her childhood and "Perfectly Contented" could represent her adulthood and maturity.**	**Answers will vary.**

Lesson 1.5 Characterization

Sample answers are in bold.

Dictionary Definition of Characterization: **The act of describing the character or qualities of someone or something.**		Group's Definition: **Answers will vary.**
Question	**Answer**	**Textual Evidence**
Describe the characteristics of Suyuan Woo and Jing-mei Woo? Consider their speech, personalities, and physical actions.	**Suyuan is bold, prideful, and a worrier, Jing-mei is stubborn, jealous, and a procrastinator.**	**Answers will vary.**

Question	Answer	Textual Evidence
Describe the characteristics of Lindo Jong and Waverly Jong. Consider their speech, personalities, and physical actions.	**Lindo is temperamental, rigid, and prideful. Waverly is action-oriented, decisive, and strategic.**	**Answers will vary.**

Lesson 1.5 Metaphor

Sample answers are in bold.

Dictionary Definition of Metaphor: **A word or phrase for one thing that is used to refer to another thing in order to show or suggest that they are similar.**		Group's Definition: **Answers will vary.**
Question	**"Two Kinds"**	**"Rules of the Game"**
Identify metaphors found in each chapter.	**Answers will vary; students may list the piano.**	**Answers will vary; students may list the wind.**
Explain the significance of the metaphors identified above and why they are important to the text's central theme. Use textual evidence to support your response.	**Answers will vary; students may note that the piano is called a "shiny trophy" at the end of the chapter, which is important to the theme of acceptance.**	**Answers will vary; students may note that the wind is significant because this is what Waverly uses to defeat her opponents. The wind represents her internal strength, which her mother taught her.**

Lesson 2.1 *Musée des Beaux Arts* Analysis

Sample answers are in bold.

Question	Analysis	Textual Evidence
What is the poem's rhyme scheme?	**Stanza 1:** **ABCADEDBFCFCE** **Stanza 2: AABCDDBC**	**Answers will vary.**
What is the author's tone?	**Unemotional**	**Line 11**
What do the first four lines of the poem mean?	**Answers will vary; students may infer that people go about their lives unnoticed.**	**Lines 1–4**
What examples of symbolism can you find in the poem?	**Answers will vary; students may list the ship and Icarus.**	**Stanza 2**
How is human nature portrayed in the poem?	**Humans are unaware and unconcerned with those or things around them.**	**Stanza 2**
Identify three literary devices found in the poem.	**Answers will vary.**	**Answers will vary.**

Question	Analysis	Textual Evidence
What are three questions you have about this poem? Generate three questions to address during class discussion.	Answers will vary.	

Lesson 2.1 *Landscape With the Fall of Icarus* Analysis

Sample answers are in bold.

Question	Analysis	Textual Evidence
What is the poem's rhyme scheme?	**Free verse**	**No specific rhyme scheme.**
What is the author's tone?	**Precise**	**No punctuation is used to incite inflection to the reader.**
Why is it ironic that Williams chose to use springtime as the season?	**Icarus is dying during a time of rebirth.**	**Stanzas 2–3.**
What do the last six lines of the poem mean?	**Farmers are going about their lives and do not notice what is happening around them.**	**"A splash quite unnoticed."**
What examples of symbolism can you find in the poem?	**Answers will vary. Students may list Icarus and the sun**	**Lines 1, 5, 6**
How is human nature portrayed in the poem?	**Answers will vary; students may note that humans seem preoccupied.**	**Stanza 5**
Identify three literary devices found in the poem.	**Answers will vary.**	**Answers will vary.**
What are three questions you have about this poem? Generate three questions to address during class discussion.	**Answers will vary.**	

Lesson 2.3 Greek Gods and Goddesses

Sample answers are in bold.

God/Goddess	Symbol	Weapon	Flaw
Aphrodite	**Love, beauty, pleasure**	**Dove/mirror**	**Loyal**
Apollo	**Music, poetry, art**	**Lyre/bow and arrow**	**Defender**
Ares	**War**	**Spear/helmet/vulture**	**Aggressive**
Artemis	**Hunt, archery, the moon**	**Hunting dog/stag/bow and arrow**	**Sensitive**
Demeter	**Agriculture, fertility**	**Wheat/torch/bread**	**Emotional**

God/Goddess	Symbol	Weapon	Flaw
Hermes	Trade, travelers, athletes	Lyre/rooster	Cunning
Hera	Marriage, women, birth, the heavens	Scepter/pomegranate	Jealous
Hades	King of the Underworld	Drinking horn/scepter	Selfish
Poseidon	Ruler of the seas, earth-quakes, storms, horses	Trident/fish/horse/bull	Arrogant
Zeus	Rules over the skies, thun-der, lightning, order	Thunderbolt/set of scales	Temperamental

Lesson 2.4 Symbolism and Theme

Sample answers are in bold.

Symbol	Meaning	Textual Evidence
The Land of the Dead	Hell or a place of regret/justice for those who committed acts on Earth	Book 11
Odysseus's Bow	Redemption	Books 22–23
The Sea	Obstacles	Book 13
Ithaca	Home; life	Book 22–23
Athena	Ally; mentor	Book 22
Theme		
Tragic Flaw *Find examples of this theme in the text, and explain it using Odysseus's characteristics and actions.*	Answers will vary. Students should understand that Odysseus leaves home for glory, treasure, and honor, which all resulted in obstacles preventing his return home.	

Lesson 2.5 Poetry Analysis

Sample answers are in bold.

Understanding the Text	Response	Textual Evidence
Choose one type of literary device and explain its signif-icance to "Siren Song." How does imagery add to the use of symbolism within the poem?	Answers will vary; students may mention symbols such as the bird suit, beached skulls, and the picturesque island. The island lends itself to beauty and mystery, which makes it irresist-ible just like the song sang to the men by the Sirens.	Stanzas 1–5
How does "Ithaka" imitate *The Odyssey*?	Ithaka is the reality that Odysseus left behind. The poem sets the stage for Odysseus's journey.	Stanza 1

Understanding the Text	Response	Textual Evidence
Identify the audience for each poem. Who are the speakers and why are they important to the poems?	**Answers will vary. Students should realize that the speaker in "Siren Song" is one of the sirens; the speaker in "Ithaka" is unknown.**	**Last three stanzas; Stanza 3**
How did each piece contribute to your understanding of *The Odyssey*?	**Answers will vary.**	

Lesson 3.1 SOAPStone Analysis

Sample answers are in bold for "I've Been to the Mountaintop" by Dr. Martin Luther King, Jr.

SOAPSTone	Explanation	Textual Evidence
Speaker Who is the speaker?	**Dr. Martin Luther King, Jr.**	**King is giving the speech.**
Occasion When was the speech written and why?	**April 1968; the speech is in response to the Memphis Sanitation Strike and discusses issues of social injustice and racial inequality toward people of color, including the sanitation workers.**	**Students should make references to lines in the speech that refer to sanitation workers, social injustice, and racial inequality.**
Audience Who is the intended audience?	**Sanitation workers; the public; government**	**"They very seldom got around to mentioning the fact that one thousand, three hundred sanitation workers are on strike, and that Memphis is not being fair to them . . ."**
Purpose What is the reason behind the speech?	**King uses the speech to convey his visions of America and racial inequality through the use of his own experiences and biblical allusions.**	**"The issue is injustice. The issue is the refusal of Memphis to be fair and honest in its dealings with its public servants . . ."**
Subject What is the topic?	**Learn from the past and from each other**	**Students should reference items referring to past historical figures.**
Tone What is the author's tone?	**Optimistic**	**"We have an opportunity to make America a better nation . . ."**

Lesson 3.2 Persuasive Language Analysis

Sample answers are in bold.

Persuasive Elements of Writing	Argument Against King's Plight According to the Clergy	Argument for King's Plight According to King
Pathos: Audience Appeal	**Answers will vary. Students may note the clergymen appeal to their audience, noting their "heavy responsibility" and that they "speak in a spirit of humility."**	**Answers will vary. Students may note that King appeals to the clergymen "as a fellow clergyman and a Christian brother."**
Logos: Logic of Breaking the Law and Getting Arrested	**Answers will vary. Students may note that the clergymen "urge those who strongly oppose desegregation to pursue their convictions in the courts" and that "these demonstrations are unwise and untimely."**	**Answers will vary. Students may note that King believes the clergymen ignore the "conditions that brought about the demonstrations."**
Ethos: Credibility	**Answers will vary. Students may note that the clergymen believe that "decisions of those courts should in the meantime be peacefully obeyed."**	**Answers will vary. Students may note that King outlines four steps of nonviolent protest: "collection of the facts to determine whether injustices exist, negotiation, self-purification, and direct action." He also notes the facts, that Birmingham has "more unsolved bombings of Negro homes and churches" than any city.**

Lesson 3.3 Civil Rights Concept Organizer

Sample answers are in bold.

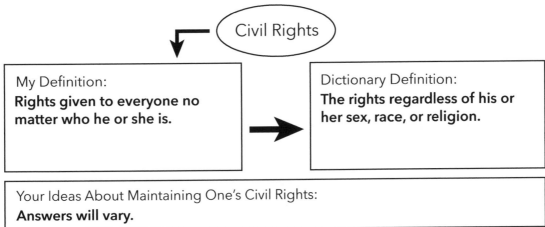

Civil Rights

My Definition:
Rights given to everyone no matter who he or she is.

Dictionary Definition:
The rights regardless of his or her sex, race, or religion.

Your Ideas About Maintaining One's Civil Rights:
Answers will vary.

| Example: **Hiring a person because of her skill.** | Historical Figures Who Advocated for Civil Rights: **Dr. Martin Luther King, Jr. Nelson Mandela Rosa Parks Jesse Jackson** | Related Words/Phrases: **Affirmative Equal Freedom Nonviolent** |
| Nonexample: **Refusing to hire a person because she is a woman.** | | |

A Sentence Using the Phrase *Civil Rights*:
It is my civil right to speak at this assembly.

Lesson 3.5 Poetry Analysis

Sample answers are in bold.

Theme and Content	Response	Textual Evidence (Include Stanza's Number)
What is the author's overall theme?	**Inequality in the American Dream**	**Answers will vary.**
What is the author's tone?	**Frustration during the beginning of the poem and hopeful toward the end**	**Stanza 3, 9**
Identify two types of literary devices used in the poem.	**Answers will vary. Students may identify repetition and alliteration.**	**Lines 5, 10**
What types of imagery are found in the poem?	**Answers will vary. Students may identify sight and touch.**	**"Slavery's scars;" "dog eat dog;" "grab the land;" "grab the gold."**

Theme and Content	Response	Textual Evidence (Include Stanza's Number)
What is the moral of the poem?	**Answers will vary.**	
Do you believe that Dr. Martin Luther King, Jr. would agree with Langston Hughes's views? Why or why not?	**Answers will vary.**	

Lesson 4.1 Censorship Concept Organizer

Sample answers are in bold.

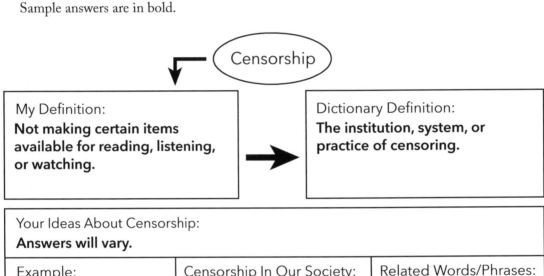

Censorship

My Definition:
Not making certain items available for reading, listening, or watching.

Dictionary Definition:
The institution, system, or practice of censoring.

Your Ideas About Censorship:
Answers will vary.

Example: **Suppression of language in a movie.**	Censorship In Our Society: **Music** **Movies** **Language** **Books**	Related Words/Phrases: **Control** **Suppress** **Unacceptable** **Selective**
Nonexample: **Nonsuppression of language in a movie.**		

A Sentence Using the Word *Censorship*:
The Nazis used censorship in many ways during World War II, including burning books.

Lesson 4.1 Dystopian Society Concept Organizer

Sample answers are in bold.

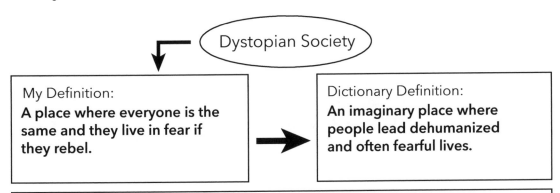

My Definition: **A place where everyone is the same and they live in fear if they rebel.**		Dictionary Definition: **An imaginary place where people lead dehumanized and often fearful lives.**

Your Ideas About Dystopian Society:
Answers will vary.

Example: **Panem (*The Hunger Games*)**	Books or Short Stories About Dystopian Society: ***Anthem*** **"Harrison Bergeron"** ***The Hunger Games*** ***1984*** ***Brave New World*** ***The Giver***	Related Words/Phrases: **Restricted** **Controlled** **Uniformed**
Nonexample: **United States**		

A Sentence Using the Phrase *Dystopian Society*:
Katniss Everdeen lived in a dystopian society.

Lesson 4.1 Understanding the Text

Sample answers are in bold.

Understanding the Text	Response	Textual Evidence
What does the title of the novel symbolize?	**The title symbolizes the kindling point of paper.**	Self-evident
Choose one type of literary device, such as symbolism, imagery, or metaphor, and explain its significance to the novel or character(s).	**Answers will vary.**	**Answers will vary.**
What examples of conflict are shown in the novel? Choose two types of conflict, such as man vs. man, man vs. himself, man vs. nature, or man vs. society. Explain their significance to the main character's situation.	**Answers will vary. The novel contains many forms of conflict. Students must connect the conflict to the character's situation.**	**Answers will vary.**
What is the overall theme?	**Censorship**	**Answers will vary.**

Understanding the Text	Response	Textual Evidence
Which type of characterization, direct or indirect, can be found within the novel, and how does the selected characterization contribute to the understanding of the novel's theme?	**Answers will vary. Both types of characterization may be found within the novel and students must make the determination and connection to the theme**	Answers will vary.
What is the significance of books, according to Beatty?	Answers will vary.	Answers will vary.
Think about Montag and Mildred's relationship and Montag's friendship with Clarisse. How are Clarisse and Mildred different? Describe the differences in the two relationships.	Answers will vary.	Answers will vary.
Think of the characteristics of the "television wall." Do we have a version of a "television wall" within our society?	Answers will vary.	Answers will vary.
Describe the characteristic attributes of Montag, Faber, and Beatty with regard to books, magazines, and/or newspapers. What do they say? How do they act? What do they look like? What are their feelings?	Answers will vary.	Answers will vary.

Lesson 4.2 Tolerance Concept Organizer

Sample answers are in bold.

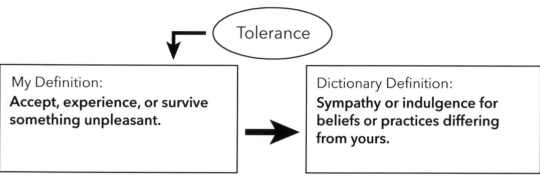

My Definition:
Accept, experience, or survive something unpleasant.

Dictionary Definition:
Sympathy or indulgence for beliefs or practices differing from yours.

Your Ideas About Tolerance:
Answers will vary.

Example: **Having patience in a long line in the cafeteria.**	Places and/or Ways You Have Shown Tolerance to Others: **Movies Grocery store School bus Hallways Classroom**	Related Words/Phrases: **Patience Steady Resistance Docility**
Nonexample: **Intolerance**		

A Sentence Using the Word *Tolerance*:
Long lines really test my tolerance.

Lesson 4.3 Propaganda Concept Organizer

Sample answers are in bold.

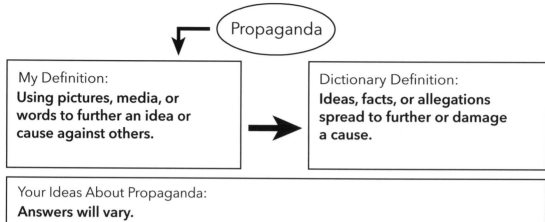

My Definition:	Dictionary Definition:
Using pictures, media, or words to further an idea or cause against others.	**Ideas, facts, or allegations spread to further or damage a cause.**

Your Ideas About Propaganda:
Answers will vary.

Example: **Political cartoons Political campaigns**	A Propaganda Drawing for Something You Would Like to Change: **Answers will vary.**	Related Words/Phrases: **Hype Publicity Indoctrination Brainwashing Advertisement**
Nonexample: **Showing someone facts or reality of a situation.**		

A Sentence Using the Word *Propaganda*:
During WWII, the government used propaganda posters to encourage the purchase of war bonds.

Lesson 4.4 Understanding the Text

Sample answers are in bold.

Understanding the Text	Response	Textual Evidence
What does the title of the novel symbolize?	**The title symbolizes the Nazis' attempts to ban and burn books.**	**Self-evident**
Choose one type of literary device, such as symbolism, imagery, or dialogue and explain its significance to the story's character(s). Explain the importance of Death as the narrator of this novel.	**Answers will vary. Students may note that Death is the narrator and is shown through many facets of the book. Death is inescapable and means different things to different characters.**	**"I do not carry a sickle or scythe. I only wear a hooded black robe when it's cold . . . You want to know what I truly look like? . . . Find yourself a mirror . . ."**

Understanding the Text	Response	Textual Evidence
Which examples of conflict are shown in this novel? Choose two types of conflict, such as man vs. man, man vs. himself, man vs. nature, or man vs. society. Explain their significance to the main character's situation.	Answers will vary. There are various types of conflict found within the text. Students must connect their choice to the main character Liesel or any other significant character within the text (Hans, Rudy, or Max).	Answers will vary.
What is the overall theme of the novel?	Showing courage during adversity.	Answers will vary.
Which type of characterization, direct or indirect, can be found in the novel, and how does the selected characterization contribute to the understanding of the novel's theme?	Answers will vary. Students must choose between indirect and direct characterization and connect their choice to the novel's theme. Both types of characterization are present in the novel.	Answers will vary.